VIKING AGE BREW

The Craft of Brewing Sahti Farmhouse Ale

Mika Laitinen

CHICAGO
REVIEW
PRESS

To all who have helped keep the
farmhouse brewing traditions alive.

Published by Chicago Review Press Incorporated
814 North Franklin Street
Chicago, Illinois 60610
ISBN 978-1-64160-047-7

Library of Congress Cataloging-in-Publication Data
Names: Laitinen, Mika, author.
Title: Viking age brew : the craft of brewing sahti farmhouse ale / Mika
    Laitinen.
Description: Chicago, Illinois : Chicago Review Press Incorporated, [2019] |
    Includes bibliographical references and index.
Identifiers: LCCN 2018061301 (print) | LCCN 2019000669 (ebook) | ISBN
    9781641600484 (PDF edition) | ISBN 9781641600507 (EPUB edition) | ISBN
    9781641600491 (Kindle edition) | ISBN 9781641600477 (trade pbk. edition)
Subjects: LCSH: Sahti—Amateurs' manuals. | Brewing—Amateurs' manuals.
Classification: LCC TP578 (ebook) | LCC TP578 .L45 2019 (print) | DDC
    663/.3—dc23
LC record available at https://lccn.loc.gov/2018061301

Cover design: Preston Pisellini
Cover image: Courtesy of Sami Brodkin
Interior design: Jonathan Hahn

Printed in the United States of America
5 4 3 2 1

CONTENTS

Part II | The Craft of a Farmhouse Brewer

Part III | In Your Kitchen or Brewery

FOREWORD

BY RANDY MOSHER

B EER HAS A VERY ANCIENT and fascinating place in the DNA of human society. Today we have evidence of brewing prior to the advent of agriculture, in the Neolithic period. At a site called Göbekli Tepe in eastern Turkey, evidence shows that people were brewing in quantities sizable enough to attract folks from across the region for periodic feasts. Once assembled, far-flung members of their group could trade goods, find mates, celebrate a spiritual life, and likely collapse, happy and satiated with food and enlivened by the magical ecstasy of beer. Such gatherings may have been the first wide-scale coalescing of nomadic peoples in the Near East, enticing them to settle into a farming life and begin the project of creating civilization.

Beer is in our cultural lifeblood, not just in Western societies but in Asia, Africa, and the Americas as well. Over the ages beer has served us admirably. It's a humble servant: offering much, asking little, and playing many roles. Beer can be quenching, filling, relaxing, thrilling, comforting, uniting, and thought provoking. All from a few seeds of grass and some flavorful herbs, transformed by the magic of yeast. Oh yes, and the staggering ingenuity of the human mind.

All of these qualities shine through in the remnants of a near-vanished tradition: Nordic farmhouse brewing. In places where the modern world has for whatever reason not fully penetrated, a few steadfast artisans are carrying on the old ways, serving their communities in celebration or grief with fresh, tasty, and uplifting ales, just as they have for untold ages. Their tools and methods are simple, but the results are profound.

Beer today is undergoing a creative explosion unlike anything in its seventeen-thousand-year history. Artisanal brewers across the planet are bringing their ideas into liquid reality, and thanks (or curses) to the Internet, the pace is accelerating at a frightening rate. At the core of this revolution, however inventive, is a reimagining of the old ways. There is nothing really ever novel in art, just a recycling of previous ideas in new contexts. This mix of old and new creates a tension that can be the engine of art—one reason why we care so deeply about it.

Just as heirloom plants add their DNA to the betterment of cultivated species, allowing them to adapt to changed conditions and needs, beer's history serves a reservoir of ideas, tastes, and techniques for creative minds to draw from as they create something uniquely suited to the moment.

The rustic and delicious farmhouse ales covered in this book are jewels of our cultural heritage, and they deserve to be cherished for that reason alone. But they also connect us directly to other human beings over the vast gulf of thousands of years. In their presence we find ourselves face to face with our past and ready to write the next amazing chapter of our history.

ACKNOWLEDGMENTS

IN 2013 I ASKED MY GOOD FRIEND Johannes Silvennoinen to join me in writing an article about sahti. He needed some time to think but a week later replied, "Let's write a book." Mutual friend Hannu Nikulainen soon joined the team, and we began a journey that would put us in touch with dozens of farmhouse brewers all over Finland and Estonia. Our Finnish-language book on sahti came out in 2015. The book you are now holding is not a translation of the Finnish work but did spring from those beginnings. Thanks to Johannes and Hannu, I still haven't drained the well of stories, even after two whole books on sahti.

The farmhouse brewers in the Nordic and Baltic countries who have contributed by sharing their craft with me are far too numerous to mention, but I wish to acknowledge the following people in particular, who have on multiple occasions dedicated several hours to explaining what they do: Jørund Geving, Morten Granås, Simonas Gutautas, Kari Harju, Veli-Matti Heinonen, Pekka Kääriäinen, Kauko Kuusikko, Petteri Lähdeniemi, Seppo Lisma, Paavo Pruul, Heikki Riutta, Roar Sandodden, Ilkka Sipilä, Hannu Sirén, Lars Andreas Tomasgård and his brewing crew in Hornindal, Eila Tuominen, Hannu Väliviita, Olavi Viheroja, and Jouko Ylijoki.

In addition, many members of the international beer community have been incredibly helpful. Special thanks go to Lars Marius Garshol, who has never tired of discussing beer traditions with me and has greatly enhanced my understanding of cereal beverages. I am also grateful to Martyn Cornell and Merryn Dineley, for their valuable comments for the "History of Farmhouse Ales" chapter. Randy Mosher too deserves thanks, for a foreword that summarizes well the importance of getting the word out about northern farmhouse ales.

I have been most fortunate to work with exceptional photographers and language professionals. Thanks are due Sami Perttilä, Sami Brodkin, and Jyrki Vesa, for providing outstanding photos that added dimension to this story. Sometimes I have difficulties in putting my thoughts down in words, but editor Anna Shefl applied a wizard's touch to read my mind and take the text of the book to the next level. I am indebted to Teijo Aflecht for looking over the book proposal and to Juha Virkki for his sage advice on publishing. Finally, the Chicago Review Press team did excellent work guiding this book over the finish line.

The greatest thanks, however, are reserved for my wife and best friend, Mari Varonen. Without her love and support I wouldn't be who I am today and probably would never even have started writing about beer.

— I —

Tradition, Culture, and History

A historical brewing demonstration at the Medieval Market of Turku, 2016. COURTESY OF SAMI BRODKIN

⊸ I ⊸

An Introduction to Farmhouse Ales

A Few Sips and the Bigger Picture

I N DAYS GONE BY, European farmers brewed beer from their own grains. This was a drink made by the people, for the people. They prepared the grains themselves, added flavors that grew nearby, and fermented the brew with yeast that was in their family. The brewers were regular farming folk who passed on the craft by word of mouth.

In the first millennium, such farmhouse traditions formed the primary way of brewing in Europe. Later, these domestic traditions were superseded, from the twelfth century onward, by beer that was produced more professionally and efficiently. By the twentieth century, preindustrial-style farmhouse brewing had all but disappeared from Europe. It remained in only a few isolated places.

A primitive form of farmhouse brewing was preserved in a few of the northernmost countries in Europe. This created *sahti* in Finland, *koduõlu* in Estonia, *gotlandsdricke* in Sweden, *maltøl* in Norway, and the *kaimiškas* beers of Lithuania. Sahti is the best known, but these are all part of the same extended family of ancient farmhouse ales.

These ales are the best surviving examples of what European beer was like before professionally brewed hopped beer became common-place in the late Middle Ages. Although farmhouse brewing traditions

This sahti master, Eila Tuominen, learned the traditional brewing methods by assisting her mother. Her mother, in turn, learned to make sahti in the same way. Nobody knows when exactly it all started. MIKA LAITINEN

3

underwent partial modernization in the twentieth century, they still offer a fascinating view of brewing in the Middle Ages and the Viking Age.

Ancient ales are sometimes re-created via fragmented information from archaeological finds and historical texts, supplemented with educated guesses about forgotten crafts. What the surviving farmhouse ales such as sahti bring to the table are practical methods that work without thermometers, stainless steel, or modern brewer's yeast. As a bonus, sahti and its cousins can even give hints of what medieval ale tasted like, and I can be quite certain that at times it tasted pretty darned good! Admittedly, the primitive folk ales of today aren't a time machine that can take us directly back to how things were a thousand years ago, but in this book I will argue that they can come close.

A few breweries in northern Europe have scaled up and commercialized the old domestic farmhouse techniques, but these folk beers are rarely exported, and they can be hard to find even in their homelands. However, this is only a small obstacle to tasting fresh malty farmhouse ale that is unlike any industrial beer sold today. Sahti is a traditional form of homebrewing, and here I will unlock the doors to brewing sahti and other ancient ales, whether you are new to brewing or an experienced brewer.

In midwinter the sahti heartland gets only five to six hours of natural light per day. Little wonder that the shortest day of the year marks the high point for northern farmhouse ales. Still today, having plenty of the finest ale ready on December 21 is a matter of honor for a thousand or so traditional Nordic and Baltic brewers.

Before embarking any further, I should clarify that today "farmhouse ale" refers to beers that have their roots in farms but are not necessarily brewed on farms. It is a very generic term—at one time, most beer in Europe was farmhouse ale, after all. Therefore, the term does not describe a particular beer style, nor is it bound to any specific country, ingredient, or brewing technique.

Everyday and Feast Ales

Farmhouse ales have been made in different strengths for different purposes. In wide stretches of northern Europe, low-alcohol ales used to be part of the diet and drunk by everyone, children included. At feasts, however, the ale was expected to be heady and rich in taste. In Nordic farmhouses of yore, the idea of a feast without ale would have been as ridiculous as that of a pub with no beer.

Besides the alcohol content, this division had a notable effect on ingredients and brewing techniques. Everyday ales were easy and economical to brew on a weekly basis for the whole household, while at northern European feasts, both the quality and the quantity of the ale were a matter of pride. As recently as the 1960s, weddings in the districts where sahti thrived were celebrated for several days, and the last drops of this drink practically marked the end of the feast.

Sahti and its closest relatives are clearly feast ales, with an alcohol content typically in the range of 5–9 percent. Even today, sahti is usually made for special events such as Christmas celebrations or weddings. Surely the character of the feasts and the associated drinking customs have helped to preserve the traditions.

Low-alcohol farmhouse ales, on the other hand, are largely extinct, or heavy-handedly modernized. Actually, what I call here everyday ales or low-alcohol ales haven't always been beers: some versions were sour fermented cereal beverages that contained no alcohol to speak of. Nevertheless, traditional cereal drinks such as *kvass* in Eastern Europe, *kalja* in Finland, *kali* in Estonia, *gira* in Lithuania, and *svagdricka* in Sweden reveal interesting facts about the prehistory of beer. While this book mostly discusses feast ales, I will briefly delve into this much overlooked side of beer traditions in the chapter "Low-Alcohol Farmhouse Ales" (page 95).

The most traditional way of enjoying sahti is from a wooden *haarikka*, which is intended to be shared.
MIKA LAITINEN

In addition, there are medium-strength farmhouse ales, which bring a smile to the lips but do not stop the work. Such ales were served, for example, during communal work in which the workers were unpaid but provided with beer. Any such distinction in terms of strength becomes blurred in some regions, however—at least these days when the flavorful premium version is drunk more often. While most sahtis even today are deceptively strong, at 7 to 9 percent alcohol, Lithuanian farmhouse ales, for example, are typically very drinkable at around 6 percent.

Geography

The most noteworthy remnants of ancient European farmhouse ales alive today are found in the Nordic and Baltic regions. The Nordic countries are Denmark, Finland, Iceland, Norway, and Sweden. Sometimes these countries are together referred to as Scandinavia, but the most prevalent definition of Scandinavia includes only Denmark, Norway, and Sweden. The Baltic region is formed by Estonia, Latvia, and Lithuania. All these countries are linked by the Baltic Sea, which throughout history has been an important route of immigration, trade, and warfare. Through the

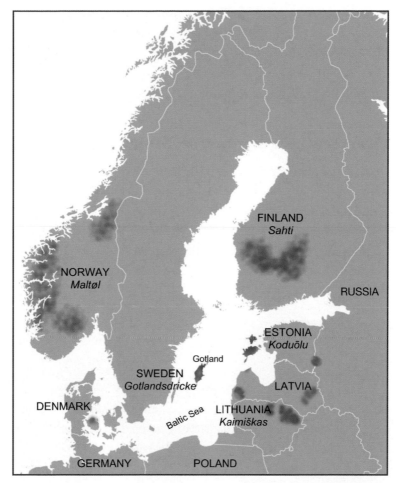

The Nordic and Baltic countries, and the main areas where farmhouse ale traditions remain alive. Once sahti was commonly found across western Finland, but now it is a regional specialty. MIKA LAITINEN

expansion of the Vikings in AD 800–1050, the Nordic influence can be seen in, for example, the British Isles and Russia. While the Vikings are usually thought of as Scandinavians, apparently some Finns joined them, and there were Baltic tribes on the coast of the Baltic Sea that lived much as the Vikings did.

The map of surviving farmhouse brewing traditions is still being honed in 2018. The domestic brewers do not always make a noise about themselves, and nobody can claim to be fully aware of all areas with living traditions. Evidently, farmhouse brewing has survived also in Latvia, but little is known about it. In Sweden, farmhouse brewing is alive only on the island of Gotland. In Denmark, the traditions faded relatively recently, but at least one brewer still practices the ancient craft. Some kind of farmhouse brewing is alive in parts of Russia as well, at least in the republic of Chuvashia and the Perm Krai region.

An Overview of Farmhouse Brewing

The brewing practices of the farm folk have been extremely diverse, but in essence the ancient feast ales such as sahti, koduõlu, gotlandsdricke, maltøl, and kaimiškas beer are crafted as follows.

Malted and unmalted grains, juniper branches, hops, and yeast are the basic ingredients of the northern farmhouse ales. Malted barley is the most common base grain, but rye, oats, and wheat too are used, in both malted and unmalted forms.

The most traditional farmhouse setup involves two large wooden vessels: a vat for *mashing* and another vat, or a trough-like vessel, for filtering out grain solids. In Finland, the filtering vessel is known as a *kuurna* and traditionally is made from a hollowed-out log.

Regrettably, traditional home *malting* has largely disappeared, and now most brewers use commercial malt. In Norway and Lithuania, some brewers still perform malting in the traditional way. Meanwhile, in Finland, a few farmers have revived home malting but with somewhat modernized methods.

In the Nordic and Baltic farmhouse ales, juniper is a more important brewing herb than hops. Traditionally, juniper branches are used as a filtering aid in draining the sweet liquid from the filtering vessel while leaving the grain solids behind. This gives a delicate coniferous taste somewhat different from the berries. Some brewers further enhance the flavor with a juniper infusion, created by infusing branches in hot water. If hops are used, the quantities are small, and many sahtis are unhopped.

In the old days, farmhouses had their own yeast strains for baking and brewing, sometimes using the same one for both jobs. Around 1900, commercial baker's yeast started to replace the house strains, and by the 1950s sahti was fermented predominantly with commercial baker's yeast. Some brewers in Norway and Lithuania hold on to their traditional heirloom yeasts, and some of them are still fermenting with a yeast originating from who knows when. Today most northern farmhouse brewers use baker's yeast, which gives a rustic edge to the ale, since this baking yeast has not been bred or manufactured for brewing.

Much of the character of these ales comes from the traditional brewing process, which evolved from using what farm equipment was available and relied on wooden vessels. Although many Nordic and Baltic brewers now use stainless steel equipment, their brewing practices largely follow the old ways, as if the brewing vessels were made of wood and thermometers had not been invented.

Brewing begins by mixing water with crushed grains to form a *mash*. The purpose of this step is converting grain starches to sugars, as in all brewing, but the farmhouse techniques for raising and maintaining the temperature are varied and often highly unusual. For example, many sahti brewers add water in several steps over five to eight hours, and even the ancient technique of heating the mash with hot stones is still used by a few brewers.

After this, the mash is scooped into a filtering vessel, on top of fresh juniper branches, which act as a filter. In the end, the resulting malty liquid, or *wort*, flows out of the vessel, leaving the grain solids behind.

Boiling the wort with hops became common in the late Middle Ages. It gives the beer a bitter edge, removes haze-causing proteins, and acts as a preservative, extending the life of the beer. However, this method did not gain a foothold in all northern farmhouses, since farmers could seldom afford to buy big kettles. Hence, sahti brewers would skip the wort boil altogether or instead boil their mash. An ale made from unboiled wort is hazy and does not keep well, but at its best it has an exquisite cereal-malty freshness and smooth, viscous mouthfeel. The lack of a boil is one of the main features connecting sahti with medieval and Viking Age ale. Often, traditional Nordic and Baltic brews are *raw ales*, devoid of any boiling steps.

These days, some northern farmhouse brewers do boil their wort, but the boiling time can vary wildly, from a few minutes to several hours, again creating something completely different from modern commercial beer.

Typically, these ales are fermented warm for a day or two and then transferred to a cool cellar. Often a considerable amount of residual sweetness remains, and slow secondary fermentation keeps the yeast active, protecting the drink from growing stale or souring. These ales are usually served within one to three weeks from the brewing day.

A Taste of History

Beer produced on a farmstead with wooden vats, within a week, and without a clue about brewing science? It must be sour and foul! Once I was a skeptic too, but on my travels I have tasted fine ales made with extremely archaic techniques by regular farmhouse folk. On the other hand, some archaeologists have tried to re-create ancient beers by working from just educated guesses about the processes, and failed miserably. Clearly, there is a plethora of folk wisdom within the old farmhouse brewing techniques.

The ancient brewing methods certainly bring their own taste to these ales, and the first sip of sahti may taste odd, as your very first beer did. These ales also defy classification into a particular beer style. In addition to regional differences, there is enormous variation from brewer to brewer, and even sahti from the same brewer can taste different each time, particularly on account of differences in age and storage.

Sahti is typically hazy and has a reddish-brown hue. This example has a gentle fizz, but many brews are completely still.

These ales are often turbid and have low carbonation. Sahti is often completely still. The backbone of the taste is usually in firm fresh maltiness and substantial sweetness. Typical flavors include cereals, bread, juniper, and assorted fruits and spices from the fermentation. The overall impression is of something extremely fresh, nourishing, smooth, and drinkable. The alcohol content is often deceptively hidden. Although these ales may go sour with age, sourness is usually considered a flaw or simply a sign of being too old or improperly stored.

Yes, the shelf life of these ales is short, but for someone who grew up with the tradition, that isn't a concern—the important thing is that the ale is perfect at the feast.

BREWING TERMINOLOGY

I will attempt to keep the terminology at a minimum, but these well-established brewing terms are essential in describing how beer is made.

Malt

Mixing raw cereals with hot water creates a starchy gruel that yeast cannot ferment into alcohol. Therefore, brewers need malt, which contain enzymes that are able to convert starches into sugars. The process of making it, called malting, begins with steeping the grains in water. Then, the wet grains are allowed to germinate, generating the enzymes. In nature, germination would give life to a new plant, but the maltster halts this process by drying the grains. Simultaneously, drying creates a whole spectrum of new flavors, such as bread, toffee, and honey—the tastes generally referred to as malty. The malting process is very laborious and takes at least a week, but one malting can yield a year's supply.

Except with a few special malt types, the conversion of starches to sugars occurs on the brew day when malt is mixed with hot water. Some brewers add unmalted cereals to the mix, since pale malt usually has enough enzymes to convert a considerable amount of starch from raw grain along the way.

The Brewing Process

With very few exceptions, a modern brewery is operated as follows: First, malt is mixed with hot water. This procedure is called mashing, and the mixture is the mash. Then the sweet malt-sugar-filled liquid, the wort, is drained from the mash in a process called *lautering*. The vessels in which these processes take place, in turn, are called the *mash tun* and *lauter tun*. After lautering, the wort is boiled with hops, cooled, fermented, and packaged.

The ancient farmhouse brewing process can be quite different from this, and many of the brews in this book are raw ales, where neither mash nor wort is boiled. Nevertheless, the terms above are useful.

Gravity, Alcohol Content, and Residual Extract

Farmhouse brewers rarely measure alcohol content or the property called *gravity*, but the brewing literature considers these to be fundamental measurements, and they are useful for understanding the process. The concentration of sugars in the wort is a large factor in the alcoholic strength, and brewers refer to gravity when speaking of the wort's sugar content, or, more precisely, the *extract* content. In beer, the extract consists principally of sugars, along with smaller amounts of other substances, such as proteins, extracted from the malt, unmalted cereals, and other sugar sources.

I prefer to express gravity in degrees Plato (°P), referring to the concentration of the extract in the wort as a percentage by weight. Fermentation turns the majority of the extract into alcohol, which for this book is measured in percentage alcohol by volume (ABV). Some *residual* extract remains, which gives the beer its sweetness and body, and the amount in the finished product too is measured in degrees Plato.

For example, a typical modern beer with 5 percent ABV is usually made from a 12°P gravity wort, from which 8°P from the extract is fermented into alcohol and 4°P remains in the beer as residual extract.

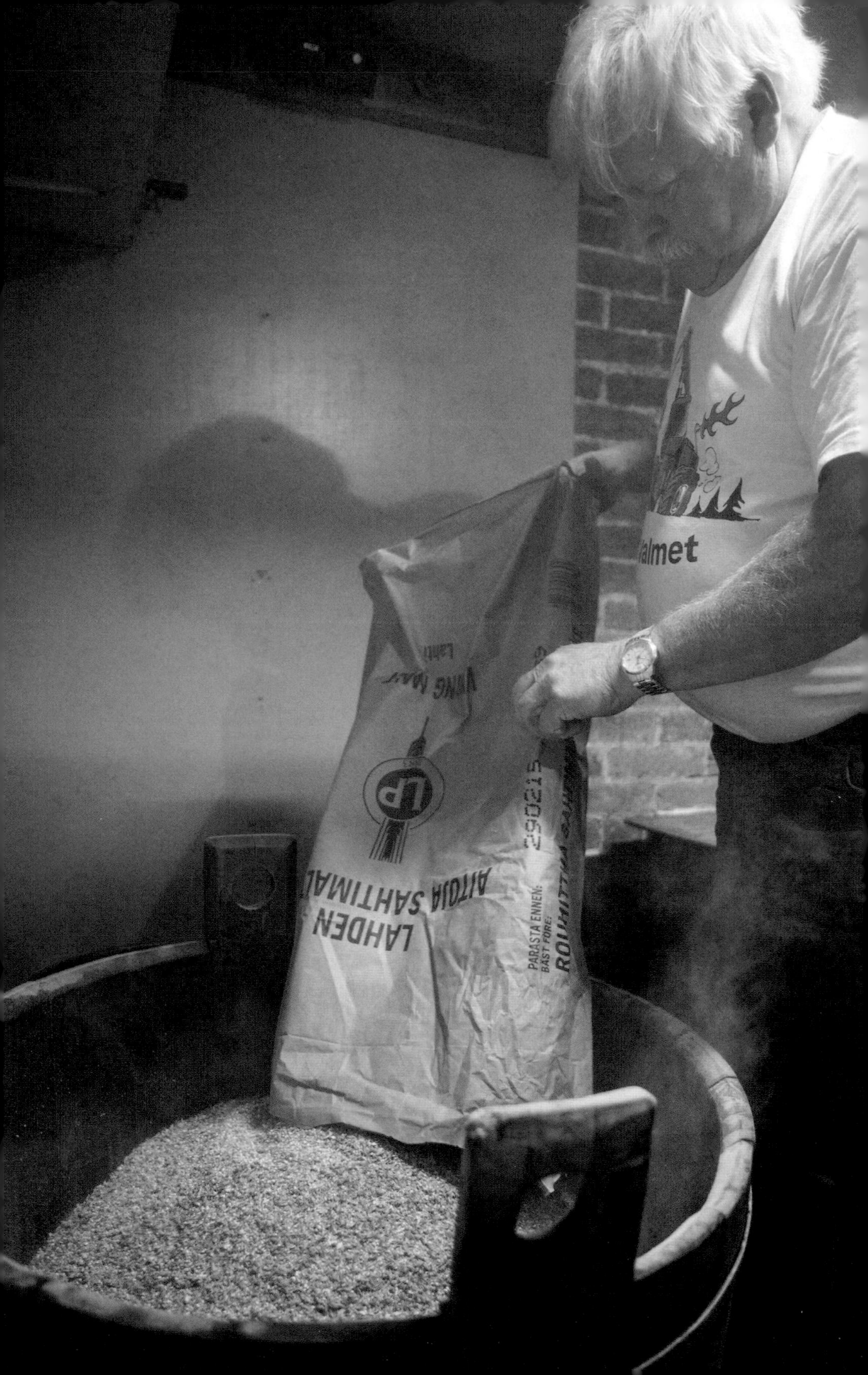
LAHDEN
PARASTA ENNEN:
BÄST FÖRE:

− 2 −

Brew Day with a Master

Learning the Craft the Traditional Way

IN AUGUST 2014 I visited renowned sahti master Hannu Sirén in the small rural municipality of Hartola. He was about to brew sahti, in the same way he has since the 1970s. This was a normal brew day for him, but for me it was a fascinating lesson in the history of beer.

About the only reminder here of modern times was a thermometer, which Hannu uses for measuring water and fermentation temperatures. This gives him more control, but he could easily brew without it.

When I walk into the one-room brewhouse, aromas of juniper and campfire touch my nose. I see a big staved wooden vat, and beside the wall rests a slightly elongated tapped vat made from a hollowed-out log. In a corner sits an iron cauldron on a wood fire, filled with water and juniper branches. I see no stainless steel as found at a modern brewery.

As most sahti brewers do, Hannu fills the bulk of his *grain bill* (the list of malted and unmalted grains in the recipe) with Sahti Malt, a commercial blend of Finnish barley malts. In traditional sahti districts such as Hartola, this malt is so common that a sackful can be picked up at the local grocery store. Hannu also malts small quantities of rye in his shed and uses some unmalted rye grown by a local farmer. For sahti his grain bill is unusually complex, and I can taste that grainy complexity in his brew.

Although the following list gives measures by weight, Hannu doesn't actually weigh his grains. Instead, he just pours an eyeballed portion from a sack or measures the grain amounts by volume with buckets.

The way Hannu Sirén brews his sahti would be called experimental archaeology in most parts of the world.

Hannu in his brewhouse. The brewing setup includes his lautering vat, called a kuurna (left); mashing vat (middle); and wood-fire-heated cauldron.

Ingredients for 25 US gallons (100 liters)*
80 lb. (40 kg) Sahti Malt
6 lb. (3 kg) dark caramel malt
5 qt. (5 L) home-malted rye
5 qt. (5 L) unmalted rye
2 qt. (2 L) wheat malt
Juniper branches
5 oz. (150 g) fresh compressed baker's yeast

* NOTE: 25 gallons does not exactly equal 100 liters, but throughout the book I use this handy trick for scaling between imperial and metric units: 2 pounds for 1 gallon (4 quarts) gives the same weight-to-volume ratio as 1 kilogram for 4 liters. This provides for easy conversion with 1 quart corresponding to 1 liter, 2 pounds to 1 kilogram, and 1 ounce to 30 grams.

Hannu prepared the juniper infusion the night before: he clipped juniper branches from nearby trees, tossed them into water, and brought the concoction to a boil. Also the day before, the wooden vats were wetted, making them watertight. The brew day begins at 6:30 AM when Hannu cleans the wooden vats with the juniper infusion.

At 7:00 AM Hannu pours malt into an empty mashing vat. Then he begins to add a mixture of heated water and juniper infusion water, poured over the malt. The liquid mix (or *liquor*) is added gradually, in five steps, and after each addition the mash rests for around forty-five minutes.

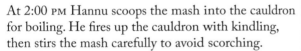

Hannu raises the mash temperature by using hotter liquor in each step. Gradually, over five hours, the mash goes from completely dry to a porridge-like liquid, and it warms from hand-warm to hot. At 12:30 PM he adds the last portion of liquor to the mash and leaves it to rest. Meanwhile, he cleans the kuurna: he pours several buckets of boiling-hot juniper infusion into it. This also guarantees that the vat will be watertight.

At 2:00 PM Hannu scoops the mash into the cauldron for boiling. He fires up the cauldron with kindling, then stirs the mash carefully to avoid scorching.

At 4:00 PM the mash begins to boil, and Hannu starts to scoop the mash into the kuurna. Juniper branches have been laid at the bottom of the kuurna to form a filter. Hannu lets the wort flow through the filter for collection while he scoops in the mash. Halfway through the scooping, he closes the drain at the bottom with a wooden tap and pours the cloudier wort back into the rest of the mash mixture still in the cauldron.

When all the mash is in the kuurna, Hannu opens the tap again and lets the clear wort start draining from it slowly. At the same time, he pours hot juniper infusion onto the mash, to get the residual malt sugars out of it. As rinsing with the infusion continues, the wort gets more diluted. Hannu tastes the runnings occasionally, and he stops the flow before the wort can get too diluted. The diluted later runnings could be collected in a separate vessel to make a lower-alcohol ale (kalja), but Hannu cares only about rich and full-bodied ales.

Hannu pours the wort into old milk cans, and he lifts these into a water bath for cooling.

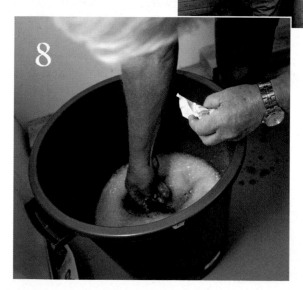

At 7:00 PM the wort has cooled down to fermentation temperature, around 73°F (23°C), and Hannu pours the wort into a plastic tub, crumbles in the baker's yeast, and covers the tub with a newspaper.

Hannu's sahti will be ready in two weeks, but Hannu likes it best at three or four weeks.

At this point, I had followed the brew for twelve hours and enjoyed a few pints from Hannu's previous batch of sahti. I had to leave, but Hannu told me how things would proceed: the vigorous fermentation in a plastic tub at warm temperatures takes around two days. Then Hannu racks the sahti into big plastic canisters and moves them into the cold. The fermentation isn't completely finished, and slower, secondary fermentation continues until serving.

Hannu's sahti has a robust taste and brings a smile. It has perhaps 8 percent alcohol by volume, but it drinks like an easygoing real ale. It shows intriguing contrasts: thick body yet easy to drink, rustic but refined, smooth yet biting, both sweet and tart. Junipery and citrussy tartness attacks smoothly, accompanied by a barrage of fresh malt and grain.

If this beer were given to someone unaware of the tradition, he or she would probably be puzzled. Is this beer? Where do these odd flavors come from?

— 3 —

The Landscape of European Farmhouse Ales

A Family Tree of Folk Beers

T RADITIONAL NORDIC AND BALTIC BREWERS often emphasize a particularly important aspect of their tradition. Interestingly, this aspect varies from region to region, and it might involve parts of the brewing process, use of wooden vessels, malting at home, or heirloom yeast. Almost nowhere in Europe has every feature of brewing remained untouched by modernity. However, if we look at the surviving farmhouse ales of Europe in combination, we can get a fairly complete picture of truly ancient brewing culture.

This is part of what makes it worthwhile to compare the living farmhouse ale traditions of Europe. It's a tricky balancing act, however. In 2018, no matter how much research has been done, nobody is fully aware of all the pockets of tradition in Europe. Even the farmhouse brewers themselves don't always recognize the diversity within their own country alone. Generalizing from highly varied traditions has its own challenges, and inevitably there will be plenty of exceptions.

The following observations are based on gut feelings arising from my travels in Finland, Estonia, Norway, and Lithuania, as well as the available literature. This is a brief survey concentrating on the most distinctive features and what has survived to the present day. The alcohol-content figures are only estimates, since farmhouse brewers don't usually measure

Remoteness and rugged landscapes are typical of farmhouse brewing hubs. Hornindal, Norway, is the epitome of this. MIKA LAITINEN

21

gravities. Finally, most of these farmhouse brews are so low on hops that I find speaking of bitterness units irrelevant.

Finland's Sahti

High malt content is the norm in the traditional feast ales, but in sahti the amount of cereal per volume of ale is perhaps the highest I have encountered in farmhouse ales. (At least on average; in all the Nordic and Baltic countries, there are brewers who push the malt content to the limit.) Usually sahti finishes sweet with lots of residual malt sugars, which keeps the alcohol content typically at 7 to 9 percent. A thick viscous mouthfeel from high residual extract levels is certainly a hallmark of sahti.

Sahti need not contain any rye, but often there is a noticeable rye taste, which distinguishes sahti from the neighboring farmhouse ales. Also, including unmalted cereals seems to be more typical among Finns.

Sahti brewers mash unusually intensively and archaically, while this seems to be rarer elsewhere in northern Europe. Luckily, the brewers

The kuurna style of lauter tun is the norm for sahti brewers but rare outside Finland.

are reluctant to alter the process, although modern malt would allow doing so.

Finland is the only country where most farmhouse brewers rely on a single yeast brand. Their choice is Suomen Hiiva's baker's yeast. Admittedly, this narrows the flavor profiles of fermentation, but this yeast has a lot of character, and it can be used in a vast number of ways. Nordic and Baltic farmhouse ales are not hoppy beers, and sahti is perhaps the least hoppy of them all.

Sahti got a head start on international recognition, since it was already mentioned in Michael Jackson's *The World Guide to Beer* in 1977, and the first commercial sahti breweries were founded in the late 1980s. Today Lithuania has more commercial examples of farmhouse-style brewing, but that country was less known for its farmhouse ales until the latter part of the 2010s. As of 2018 Finland has six commercial sahti breweries, but the most colorful examples come from hundreds of homebrewers in the countryside.

Estonia's Koduõlu

Finnish and Estonian are closely related Finno-Ugric languages—separate from the Indo-European branch of the language family, which gave rise to most European languages. This relationship has created a strong kinship between the Finns and the Estonians.

When I met farmhouse brewers on the Estonian islands of Saaremaa and Hiiumaa, I was struck by the similarities in the brewing process, ingredients, vocabulary, and drinking customs. The Estonian farmhouse ale koduõlu virtually is sahti, and vice versa. Today the Estonian islands and Finnish inland countryside seem disconnected, but there must have been a strong link once, which was likely formed during the Iron Age.

In the old days, farmhouse ale was made throughout Estonia, but today the areas where that heritage remains alive are centered in the Baltic Sea islands of Saaremaa and Hiiumaa, and in Setomaa, in the southeastern part of the country. There, a small ethnic group composed of Seto people uses malt bread to produce ale more akin to the oven beers described in the chapter "Low-Alcohol Farmhouse Ales" (page 95). From discussions with Estonians, I estimate that Estonian farmhouse brewers probably number in the tens rather than the hundreds.

In the Estonian islands, koduõlu brewers are often proud of their traditional wooden vats. Jüri Šklennik from Saaremaa uses a more-than-a-century-old wooden mashing vat.

The most obvious difference between today's sahti and koduõlu is that Estonian brewers usually employ a single barley malt, usually a pale one of Pilsner or Vienna type, which gives koduõlu its typical pale straw color. On the other hand, there are some less common variants of sahti that are brewed solely from pale barley malt and closely resemble koduõlu. The islanders don't seem to use any rye or unmalted cereals.

In general, koduõlu perhaps has slightly lower malt content than sahti, but then koduõlu is fermented to be a tad drier, which raises the alcohol content to the same range, 6–8 percent. Quite a few brewers ferment with baker's yeast, but some use dry brewer's yeast.

The islanders I met had a fairly uniform way of brewing. None of the brewers boiled the mash or wort. Most were proud of using impressive heirloom wooden brewing vats, usually capable of producing 50 gallons (200 liters) of ale. Some brewers had new wooden vats fabricated in accordance with the traditional style. Two of the brewers were using secondhand stainless steel dairy vats, explaining that frequent brewing with wooden vessels had become arduous.

Jüri Metsma brewing
koduõlu at Hiiu Õlle Koda,
on the island of Hiiumaa.
This brewpub had new
brewing vats fabricated in
the traditional style.

Those brewers using wooden vats stacked a substantial quantity of juniper branches at the bottom of the lautering vat, while two brewers with stainless steel vessels omitted juniper altogether. The use of hops is more generous than in sahti, yet I sensed only a little hoppiness. Both commercial and homegrown hops were used, but some brewers insisted that the hops should be homegrown.

Juniperless versions tasted slightly softer and more rounded, but this factor didn't make a dramatic difference. In any case, the main flavors in koduõlu are of fresh malt and cereal, alongside the fruitiness from the yeast. Some versions can be somewhat tart, though not sour.

Farmhouse brewers in Estonia have traditionally been men, which is in sharp contrast with the old traditions of Finland, Scandinavia, and Anglo-Saxon England, where almost the exact opposite used to be the norm. Perhaps the gender roles were once different in Estonia, but I haven't found any evidence of this.

In 2018 a few commercial Estonian breweries produce koduõlu year-round. Farmhouse brewers may apply for a sales license, and thus true homemade koduõlu is occasionally sold at local festivals, and even in craft beer pubs.

Norwegian Maltøl

Norway has rich and highly varied farmhouse brewing traditions, yet absurdly little was known of them until the 2010s. While ethnographer Odd Nordland documented the traditions well in his book *Brewing and Beer Traditions in Norway*, published in 1969, just a few decades later the archaic brewing methods sounded more like something from *Game of Thrones* than living culture.

In the 2010s, Norwegian beer writer Lars Marius Garshol began to survey and document the traditions. He found, much to his surprise, that maltøl was still being brewed in a truly unique fashion in several isolated pockets of Norway. He learned that several hundred brewers still make this traditional Norwegian farmhouse ale. This motivated him to publish his findings online in English in his *Larsblog* and then in the Norwegian-language book *Gårdsøl: Det norske ølet*, in 2016. He opens the book with the line "This book is about the only truly Norwegian beer, a beer that few Norwegians have tasted" (my translation).

The obscurity and diversity of maltøl can be at least partially explained by geography. Western Norway, where the tradition has survived best, is littered with fjords and mountains that can make passage difficult. A century ago, influences from the outside world couldn't reach some of the villages easily.

Literally, maltøl means "malt beer." That sounds peculiar, but the word for beer, *øl*, used to refer to all kinds of fermented drinks. *Maltøl* is an umbrella term comprising diverse ales, the fruit of both geographical and brewer-specific variation. Garshol has categorized maltøl traditions into three regional styles: *kornøl*, *vossaøl*, and *stjørdalsøl*.

Kornøl is made in western Norway, in the regions of Sunnmøre and Nordfjord, north of Bergen. The term may seem redundant, since it translates to "grain beer." Nevertheless, the ingredients are commercial pale barley malt, juniper branches, hops, and the heirloom yeast *kveik*. Kornøl is typically a yellow to pale amber raw ale with an alcohol content around

6 to 8 percent. The overall impression is of a sweetish smooth-drinking ale with a good balance of fruitiness and fresh maltiness, accompanied by a gentle touch of refreshing juniper.

In June 2017, I had the pleasure of participating in a traditional kornøl brewing session in Hornindal, Norway. Apart from the use of kveik, the brewing process was similar to making some sahti and koduõlu. Even the drinking traditions were very similar, and when a drinking bowl full of øl was passed around, I certainly sensed a brotherhood. If someone were to brew kornøl and serve it as sahti or koduõlu, I would find the taste atypical but not untraditional.

The Norwegian farmhouse yeasts, kveiks, are true gems, for home-kept heirloom yeast has mostly disappeared from Europe, apart from Lithuania. Kveiks are genetically unique, and the methods of maintaining and using them are a fascinating piece of brewing folklore that remains alive (you can read more about this in chapter 9, page 121). Handling and fermenting with kveik is one of the traditions that sahti brewers have lost.

Stig Seljeset making the juniper infusion for his kornøl in Hornindal. In Norwegian farmhouse breweries, the cauldrons too are often highly traditional.
MIKA LAITINEN

Vossaøl is an ale from Voss, which is a small town northeast of Bergen. The region has plenty of active brewers who have held on to their kveiks. In essence, the ingredients are the same as in kornøl, but the process has one very special feature: the wort is boiled for several hours, often in a copper kettle over a wood fire. This boiling tradition is perhaps a few centuries old, dating from when large copper kettles became more affordable.

That kind of boil is something a sahti brewer would never do. It darkens the color to reddish brown and concentrates the wort considerably. I haven't been to Voss, but I have made a vossaøl as a homebrewer. The four-hour boil turned the wort magically from golden to reddish brown and gave a remarkably toffeeish flavor. The alcohol content of vossaøl is probably at least 8 percent, due to thickening of the wort.

Stjørdalsøl is made in Stjørdal. This small municipality near Trondheim has around fifty traditional malt houses within only a twelve-mile (twenty-kilometer) radius—surely the highest density of malt houses in the world! Each is operated by a team of five to ten homebrewers, who share the malt and brew traditional stjørdalsøl with them. So Stjørdal must have hundreds of traditional maltsters and brewers, around one maltster-brewer per hundred inhabitants.

Stjørdal's malts are dried with alder smoke, creating a result so characterful that a genuine stjørdalsøl cannot be made without it. The malting technique is very traditional and well preserved, more akin to that of Gotland than the traditional Finnish farmhouse maltings. I will compare these malting techniques in the chapter "Grain and Malt" (page 109).

When visiting Stjørdal, I was struck by the absurdly smoky yet unexpectedly drinkable taste of stjørdalsøl. The palate gets saturated with pungent yet soft alderwood smoke, counterbalanced with a fair amount of sweetness. This ale has a reddish-brown color, and the alcohol content is typically in the 6–9 percent range. Most of Stjørdal's brewers boil their wort with a small amount of hops for around one hour, but some brew raw ale with techniques very similar to those of sahti brewers. Most use baker's yeast or brewer's yeast—Stjørdal's kveiks faded away in the 1970s—but some brewers have begun using kveik from elsewhere in Norway.

Although varieties of maltøl are brewed in various other parts of Norway, less is known about them, and they don't necessarily fall into

Morten Granås remains one of the very few commercial producers of maltøl. He prepares traditional Stjørdal-style malt and brews Granås Gård Hegra Maltøl from them. Regrettably, this outstanding smoky ale is sold only at the brewery facility in Stjørdal. MIKA LAITINEN

neatly defined categories. Elsewhere in Norway, traditional home malting is rare and takes place in only a few individual locations. It seems that there's nowhere in Norway where both kveik and farmhouse malting have been preserved.

As of 2018, commercial Norwegian farmhouse ale is hard to get. Only a few small-scale brews are available very locally or temporarily. However, a new wave of commercial maltøls or maltøl-inspired ales seems to be emerging. Perhaps when you are reading this, kveik and Stjørdal's malt will not be completely obscure descriptions on beer labels.

Sweden's Gotlandsdricke

Farmhouse brewing disappeared from the mainland of Sweden some time ago, but the traditions still flourish in Gotland. Once this island was a stronghold of the Vikings and Baltic Sea traders, but it then lapsed into remoteness, which has made it a perfect haven for traditional ales.

Gotlandsdricke translates as "the drink of Gotland," and for the locals this refers to homemade beer. In Swedish grammar, the word for drink is *dricka*, while the Gotlands dialect renders it as *dricke*. Therefore, the islanders themselves prefer to call their drink *gotlandsdricke* or simply *dricke*. Confusingly, the rest of the world often uses the grammatically mainstream *gotlandsdricka*.

Unlike sahti, gotlandsdricke encompasses both daily and feast ales. In general, the alcohol content may vary from a few percentage points to above 10, but it seems that contemporary brews are inclined to be stronger feast versions, perhaps in the range of 5–9 percent.

The most distinctive feature of gotlandsdricke is the use of honey or sugar, which can cause great variation in the alcohol content. Archaeological findings suggest that Scandinavians have added honey to fermented drinks since the Bronze Age, with sugar being a modern substitute for honey. Both can be added either before or after fermentation. In the former case, the alcohol content is boosted, while in the latter case the dricke is backsweetened, sometimes just before serving. Another common approach is to sustain a slow secondary fermentation with honey or sugar. Versions using this technique can be cellared for years, and they gradually grow stronger as they age.

Today most brewers use commercial malt, but farmhouse malting is still alive, and the most traditional procedure involves drying malt in a wood-fired kiln with direct smoke, somewhat similar to the Stjørdal technique. Gotlanders like a clear taste of juniper, and they use plenty of it both in the lautering vat and for a juniper infusion. I haven't been to Gotland, so I have no firsthand knowledge of the experience. But I have interviewed several sahti brewers who have visited the island. Finnish sahti folk who have been there comment that the taste of the smoke and juniper can be pungent.

In Gotland a wort boil is common, though the boil time can vary from just a few minutes to hours. Raw ales are brewed too, but less often. The house yeasts disappeared after World War II, and now dricke is usually fermented with baker's yeast.

There have been attempts to sell commercial dricke, but the strict alcohol laws of Sweden have put a stop to this, especially because of the variability of alcohol content. It seems that in 2018 a genuine gotlandsdricke is only available homemade and in Gotland itself.

Lithuania's Kaimiškas

Lithuanian farmhouse ale, kaimiškas, is a standout among the traditional European ales, which may be connected with the country's extraordinary history. Lithuania was among the last corners of Europe to adopt Christianity, and it has never been under German or Scandinavian rule, unlike the other Nordic and Baltic countries. Yet the overall brewing processes for kaimiškas are fairly similar to those of sahti and the other related farmhouse ales.

The word *kaimiškas* means "from the countryside." These farmhouse brews tend to be highly drinkable medium-strength ales at 5 to 7 percent ABV, but a local brewmaster told me that around the town of Biržai there is a tradition of stronger ales that reach 10 percent. Typically the color ranges from yellow to amber, though dark brown variants exist.

The distinctiveness of the kaimiškas style stems largely from the extremely well-preserved local ingredients. Some brewers still have their heirloom house yeast, and some also prepare their own malt. The farmhouse maltsters favor very pale and smokeless barley malt, in contrast to the homemade malt of Norway and Gotland. Even the commercial Lithuanian malt seems to have a taste of its own, with notes of hay.

Juniper does grow in Lithuania, but for some reason it is seldom used in kaimiškas ales. Instead, hops are the main seasoning. That said, most of these beers today are malt-forward and lightly hopped. Nevertheless, the hop aroma, flavor, and bitterness can be noticeable, unlike in the other traditional Nordic and

On the hunt for farmhouse ales in Vilnius, Lithuania. At Šnekutis bar, I decided to quench my thirst with a kvass-type cereal beverage, gira. When I ordered, the staff reminded me that this beverage does not contain alcohol.
COURTESY OF MARI VARONEN

Baltic ales. Most kaimiškas recipes yield raw ales, and the hops are cooked in a small amount of water instead of the wort. Lithuanian farmhouse ales may also freely include exotic ingredients such as peas or raspberry stems, though it is difficult to say how old these traditions are.

Lithuania is an excellent destination for a beer hunter and by far the best country for sampling commercial raw ales. The country has dozens of commercial farmhouse breweries, and many of them are highly authentic scaled-up versions of domestic breweries. (Bear in mind, though, that *kaimiškas* is not an official designation, and the authenticity of the brews bearing this name may vary.) In some specialized beer bars in bigger cities, one should be able to sample dozens of well-made farmhouse ales.

Saison and Bière de Garde

When farmhouse ale is mentioned, most beer drinkers immediately think of Belgian saison or French bière de garde, largely because of the book *Farmhouse Ales* by Phil Markowski (with contributions from Tomme Arthur and Yvan De Baets). This book paints a picture of ales originally brewed domestically for the farms' own use. However, unlike sahti, the domestic folk beer traditions of Belgium and France faded a while ago, and the brewing methods as we know them today were developed by commercial breweries. Some even question whether these ales can actually be considered fruits of farmhouse culture. Undoubtedly Belgian and French farmers of the past brewed ales, but were they anything like the saison or bière de garde we enjoy today?

Belgian brewer Yvan De Baets provided the chapter "A History of Saison" for Markowski's book, and for it he interviewed people old enough to remember the domestic farmhouse brews. He has also collected more data since the book was published in 2004, and his conclusion remains that the essence of saisons came from traditional farmhouse brews, although he admits that these kinds of ales have been subject to the forces of evolution.

Frustratingly little has been written about domestic Belgian and French ales, but that is hardly surprising. Common folk have brewed for ages, but hardly anything about their traditions was written down, even if the farmhouse folks brewed at the doorsteps of industrial breweries. Perhaps there's still some evidence to be found in ethnographic texts or folk museums. The professional brewing texts that are the favorite sources of many historians and beer writers might be a poor substitute in this case. Clearly there are plenty of gaps in our view of the brews, but I do believe that De Baets has collected plausible evidence that saison can rightly be called farmhouse ale.

In any case, today's saison and bière de garde are made with a relatively modern brewing process that employs a standard wort boil with hops, and therefore they are only distant relatives of Nordic and Baltic farmhouse ales. Nevertheless, a few aspects of saisons seem to reflect common roots: some saison yeasts are derived from those of Belgian farmhouses and are used at unusually high temperatures, like Norwegian kveik. In addition, these ales have certain characteristics that are hard to pin down, because of variation from village to village and brewer to brewer.

Other European Farmhouse Ales

Alongside the aforementioned ales, eastern parts of Europe still retain a colorful bunch of ales and nonalcoholic cereal beverages with countryside roots. Traditional kvass is a fermented cereal beverage, usually made from leftover breads, rye flour, and sometimes a portion of malt. However, the traditional fermentation for this drink seems to be dominated by lactic bacteria that does not produce alcohol. Therefore, I would not call traditional kvass a beer. Modern versions of kvass that are today fairly common in Eastern Europe would be best described as soft drinks. Nevertheless, truly traditional folk ales still can be found in some rural areas of Russia, as discovered by Lars Marius Garshol during his visit to Chuvashia and Perm Krai in 2017.

Another traditional folk ale is *boza* or *bouza*, which is still brewed in parts of the Balkans, Middle East, Central Asia, and North Africa. Boza is a highly viscous and gruel-like drink that exists in both nonalcoholic and alcoholic versions. Most of today's recipes from the Balkans, Turkey, and Egypt seem to include sugar, but the traditional techniques starting with only unmalted and malted cereals have not been forgotten.

– 4 –

History of Farmhouse Ales

What Beer Was Like a Thousand Years Ago

THE HISTORY OF BEER is full of intriguing questions. What were the first beers like? What kind of beer did the Vikings drink? Was all preindustrial beer sour? Many of these questions are closely linked to the history of traditional farmhouse ales such as sahti.

What European farmers brewed for their own use has been recorded only relatively recently. For example, the first written description of sahti is found in an academic study by Carl Niclas Hellenius from 1780. At the same time, archaeological evidence is scarce, because wooden brewing gear and organic ingredients have not survived well. Nevertheless, from combining bits and pieces from ancient writings, archaeological findings, and crafts of the past, we can conclude that traditional farmhouse brewing techniques used the same best practices as Iron Age beer lovers in northern Europe.

The History of European Farmhouse Ales in a Nutshell

I will start by outlining my scenario of the evolution of European farmhouse ales. The detailed evidence will unfold in the rest of the chapter.

Archaeological finds suggest that northern Europe's most ancient beer-like drinks, made several thousand years ago, often combined dif-

Since the dawn of civilization, people have made brewing vessels, whether from clay, wood, metal, or plastic. The choice of material has played a tremendous role in the history of beer. Modern beer relies heavily on stainless steel, while the northern farmhouse ales are rooted in the times of wooden brewing gear.

ferent sugar sources, among them grains, honey, and fruits. These mixed drinks can be described roughly as hybrids of beer, mead, and wine.

Texts by Roman historians reveal that two thousand years ago Germanic and Celtic tribes were imbibing a drink clearly identified as beer. In the first century AD, Roman historian Tacitus wrote that Germanic tribes brewed beer from barley or wheat and were inclined toward feasting and getting drunk. Later in the first millennium (AD 800–1050), the Vikings made beer, especially from barley, and they too had a habit of feasting, with large quantities of beer.

In first-millennium Europe, brewing was a household craft, predominantly involving some kind of farmhouse ale. However, from the ninth century onward, more professional and larger-scale brewing was developing, especially at monasteries. In the twelfth century, large-scale commercial production of beer gained a foothold in the urban parts of continental Europe, and the use of hops instead of other brewing herbs began to spread. Boiling the wort with hops helped beer keep better, and

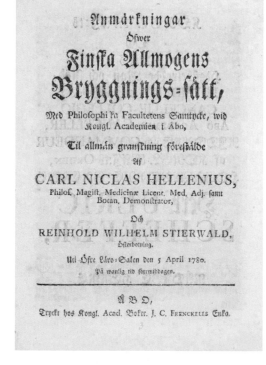

The first written description of brewing sahti, in a thesis from 1780 in which Carl Niclas Hellenius looks at brewing practices of the Finnish folk (written in Swedish). At that time, theses were more like the scientific articles of today. In his academic career, Hellenius wrote thirty-one theses. DIGITIZED BY THE NATIONAL LIBRARY OF FINLAND

by the thirteenth century brewers in towns in northern Germany were already exporting their beer to other countries. Within a few centuries, boiling the wort with hops became the norm for commercial breweries across Europe.

As this change spread early in the second millennium, the paths of farmhouse ale and urban commercial beer began to diverge. The commercial beer was often highly taxed, and competition among commercial brewers favored refinements to the brewing process, bigger investments, and larger scale. The farmhouse brewers continued to brew with archaic methods for their own use. Some countryside brewhouses invested in a copper kettle and began to boil the wort with hops.

Gradually the commercial beer made on a bigger scale began to supersede farmhouse brews, especially in the more heavily populated areas and at trade hubs. The archaic farmhouse brews survived better in more rural and remote areas. The surviving Nordic and Baltic farmhouse ales sahti, koduõlu, gotlandsdricke, maltøl, and kaimiškas beer are what remains of a much more widespread culture.

The Beginnings of Farming

The first farmers appeared in northern Europe more than six thousand years ago, but agriculture spread slowly in colder climates. In many Nordic areas, hunting, fishing, and foraging remained the main sources of food for a long time even after the arrival of grain cultivation.

In southern Scandinavia, farmhouses became the center of social life four thousand years ago, but in the harsher climates of Finland and the northern three-quarters of Scandinavia the transition took another one or two thousand years. The northernmost reaches of Finland, Sweden, and Norway are above the Arctic Circle and outside the limits for cultivation. Many parts of the Nordic and Baltic region now known for their farmhouse ales were inhabited by farmers by the beginning of the Common Era.

In the north, the primary cereal was barley right from the beginning, and in some areas oats were an important crop too. Rye wasn't among the earliest cultivated grains here, but it became common during the Viking Age. Wheat was known from early on, but it was rarely cultivated in prehistoric Nordic climes.

Interaction among people around the Baltic Sea was already commonplace at the time of early farming in this area. Scandinavian and Baltic immigrants settled in coastal Finland, especially between 500 BC and AD 500. Contacts with the Germanic and Celtic tribes of central Europe were evident early on as well—finds from burials in Denmark attest to these contacts occurring even before 1000 BC.

We don't know for sure whether the Nordic and Baltic farmers learned brewing from the Germanic or Celtic tribes, but they certainly had access to knowledge of the techniques used in Germanic and Celtic brewing.

Early Beer

Chemical analysis of ancient drink residues suggests that humankind's first beer-like drinks were often concoctions of grains, fruits, berries, honey, and herbs. This pattern is surprisingly common in archaeological finds throughout the Middle East, Asia, and Europe. In fact, the earliest direct evidence of fermented beverages comes from a nine-thousand-year-old drink residue from China, which has traces of rice, honey, and fruit.

In northern Europe, the earliest archaeological evidence of such mixed fermented drinks is from Scotland and thought to date as far back as five thousand years. Residues on pottery fragments indicate a drink made from cereals, honey, and herbs such as meadowsweet.

Starting in 1500 BC, several mixed drinks appear in Scandinavia's archaeological record. Archaeologist Patrick McGovern and his colleagues analyzed six Nordic mixed-drink residues, from 1500 BC to the first century AD. Findings from Kostræde (1100–500 BC) and Juellinge (around 200 BC), both in Denmark, are particularly interesting because the drinks were flavored with juniper. Other common herbs were bog myrtle and yarrow, which have appeared in the Nordic and Baltic farmhouse ales in recent centuries as well.

The brewing processes for these mixed drinks are largely unknown, and we can only guess why fruits, berries, and honey were so often included. Perhaps the first brewers had difficulties in making an intoxicating drink from cereal only. Berries, fruits, and honey contain wild yeast, which can get fermentation started. Honey might have been used to increase alcohol content, or to sweeten the ale just before drinking.

A birch-bark bucket unearthed from a burial in Egtved, Denmark, that was dated to 1500–1300 BC, displayed at the National Museum of Denmark in Copenhagen. The bucket once contained a mixed fermented drink, presumed to have been made from wheat, cowberries, cranberries, bog myrtle, and honey. MIKA LAITINEN

On the other hand, the drink-residue findings are usually from burials of prominent members of society, so they do not necessarily give a full picture of the first beers. Further, the number of analyzed residues is very small, considering the extent of prehistoric brewing. The first beers surely included *gruel beers* also, a sort of slightly fermented gruel. These ales can be brewed with equipment and methods far more archaic than those used for sahti, as will be shown in the chapter "Low-Alcohol Farmhouse Ales" (page 95).

In any case, it is safe to say that sahti and the related farmhouse ales are next-generation brews when compared to the first neolithic beers.

The Craft of Malting

A stronger feast ale such as sahti is made from a generous amount of malt, and arguably malting was the foremost skill of a brewer in days of yore. Malting can be done in very primitive settings, but it does require special knowledge and dedicated facilities.

Archaeologist Merryn Dineley has been searching for archaeological evidence of malting and brewing at excavations of neolithic farms in Scotland, some of them six thousand years old. According to Dineley, some of what remains is indicative of malting floors and malt-drying kilns. The floors reveal carbonized germinated grains that support this conclusion, and some of the sites feature remnants of large clay pots and fire-cracked stones, which may well be what is left of ancient brewing gear.

Dineley claims that neolithic farmers in Europe already knew the craft of malting and brewing, but the archaeological community has not yet taken the evidence to be conclusive. The neolithic farmers certainly possessed all the requisites, but archaeological evidence of the actual malting and brewing process is hard to come by in general. When germinated grains are found, it is difficult to determine with certainty whether they germinated for malting or by accident. Prehistoric constructions have seldom been identified as malting facilities.

Archaeological malting finds from Bronze Age and Iron Age Europe have been better accepted by the scientific community. In the Nordic countries, the earliest finds thought to indicate malting are from Denmark (Østerbølle, first century AD), southern Sweden (Uppåkra, fifth to seventh century AD), and the Swedish island of Öland in the Baltic Sea (Eketorp, sixth century AD). Archaeological evidence of malting from Germany and France has been dated to the fifth century BC.

In the ancient cultures of Mesopotamia and Egypt, malt was often dried in the sun, and this technique had occasionally been practiced also in northern Europe. However, in cool and moist northern climates this works only in the best weather, and it probably would not yield malt dry enough to withstand months of storage. In northern climates, even unmalted grains require additional drying before long-term storage.

Therefore, from early on, northern farmhouses have had an additional building for threshing and drying cereals after harvest. These constructions have varied greatly with time and location, but generally drying has been accomplished with some kind of hearth heated with wood and other fuels of nature. Early on, these drying facilities were employed for malting also.

Malt-drying technique has a huge impact on the flavor of a beer,

Barley of the Past

Today our beer is made mostly from barley varieties that were bred in the twentieth century for efficient malting and brewing. In the past, in contrast, brewers used heirloom grain varieties that were probably quite tasty but gave a lower yield of malt sugars. Therefore, our ancestors had to use more grain and work harder to get a heady ale. The feast ales of the past were probably slightly lower in alcohol than today's in the Nordics.

The ancient barley variety *bere* gives us a glimpse of Viking Age brewing grains. This hardy variety is still grown on the Scottish island of Orkney, and a few brewers have experimented with it. Merryn and Graham Dineley noticed at their home brewery that they needed 50 percent more bere than modern barley malt to get the same strength of beer. This drop in yield was experienced also at Swannay Brewery in Orkney. The grain variety affects the flavor too; for example, Swannay's Scapa Bere ale (only occasionally available), made solely from bere malt, had a surprisingly grainy taste reminiscent of beers made from rye malt.

and drying in the sun yields a very different taste than direct fire. Until the eighteenth century, most European malt was dried with direct fire, producing at least a slightly smoky flavor in the malt and the resulting ale. There are also old-time drying methods that do not convey a taste of smoke, such as laying malt by the oven or on a hot stone slab, but those methods are better suited to small batches of malt.

Equipment

Here's a quick math and history exercise: How much ale would a shipful of Vikings need for a feast?

The Viking warships each had a crew of around twenty-five to fifty men. I'd say they would have needed 25 to 50 US gallons (roughly 100 to 200 liters) to share among them, which is still within the range of traditional batch sizes for many Nordic and Baltic farmhouse brewers.

How to handle brewing that amount of beer with ancient equipment and techniques is not obvious. To produce 25 gallons of an ordinary ale, the mashing vessel should contain at least 25 gallons, and for stronger ales of that batch size a practical mashing vessel size would be 40 gallons. Furthermore, since grain varieties of the past yielded a lower amount of malt sugars than today's barley, brewers were probably inclined to use plenty of grains and, accordingly, large vessels.

The neolithic farms of Scotland that Merryn Dineley investigated had clay pots with a volume typically around 10 US gallons (40 liters), and these pots could have been used for mashing. Wooden trough-like

Paavo Pruul from Hiiumaa, Estonia, still brews koduõlu with these vats inherited from his grandfather. The vats are suitable for producing 25 to 50 gallons (100 to 200 liters) of ale.

vessels similar to a sahti kuurna have been crafted since the Stone Age, and they may have been used for brewing very early on.

When people learned to make staved wooden vats, crafting large brewing vessels became easier. The invention of wooden barrels is commonly attributed to the Celts of around two thousand years ago, and the craft of fashioning large staved vats must be at least that old.

Metal cauldrons were known in the Iron Age, but big metal vessels were very rare and expensive back then, so few domestic brewers could afford them. As Franz G. Meussdoerffer puts it in his *Comprehensive History of Beer Brewing*, "until the early fourteenth century wooden vats had prevailed in rural brewing and iron pots with a capacity never exceeding 600 liters [160 US gallons] were in use in the cities." Even right after the Middle Ages, a copper kettle was the most expensive tool of a brewer.

Consequently, the metal boil kettle that today is part of virtually every brewing setup wasn't a common brewer's tool at all before the second millennium. Even in the Middle Ages, domestic brewers didn't always have a large kettle or cauldron. This had a tremendous effect on the brewing techniques and the character of the beer.

The Wort Boil and Hops

Wooden brewing vessels cannot be heated externally, and an age-old method to raise the temperature in them is to add hot water or hot stones. Stones can bring liquid to a boil, but a longer boil would be troublesome—it would fill the vessel up with stones! Without a big kettle or cauldron, a pragmatic way to make wort is to heat the mash and leave the wort unboiled. With stones, it is more practical to heat the mash rather than the wort anyway.

Natural stones usually shatter from the heat shock after a few brewing sessions, so fire-cracked stones can be important markers of prehistoric brewing. Archaeologist Geir Grønnesby has excavated mounds of fire-cracked stones from several late Iron Age and medieval farmsteads in central Norway. He concluded that fire-cracked stones were common around the farmsteads of the time and are likely to have been used for brewing. In the areas examined, the piles of these stones disappeared after the sixteenth to seventeenth century. That could be due to either introduction of boil kettles or a change in drinking customs.

Some farms that regularly brewed with stones ended up with massive piles of fire-cracked stones. For example, on the site of a nineteenth-century farmhouse in Norway, shattered brewing stones filled a circular landfill area 50 yards (50 meters) in diameter and 2.3 feet (70 centimeters) deep.

Making raw ale from unboiled wort is not as rudimentary as it sounds. When at its prime, it is tasty, hearty, and nourishing. The lack of boil doesn't make the ale go sour either, as I will explain in the chapter "Drinking Sahti" (page 71). Admittedly, raw ale loses its freshness sooner than boiled-wort ale, but that doesn't become a problem if the ale is consumed quickly.

Brewing sahti in Karvia, Finland, around 1930. Apart from a few minor details, this brewing setup might as well be from the Iron Age. Note the wood-fired cauldron that is too small for boiling wort but suitable for heating water.
EINO NIKKILÄ, COURTESY OF THE FINNISH NATIONAL BOARD OF ANTIQUITIES (KANSATIETEEN KUVAKOKOELMA)

Therefore, I see plenty of reasons for most first-millennium brewers to have made raw ale. The wort boil would have been technologically difficult and expensive for them, and they probably didn't see a need for the boil either.

Hops need to be boiled at least half an hour to release their bitterness and antimicrobial compounds. It seems that the wort boil was adopted alongside the introduction of hops, as beer historian Martyn Cornell argued in his book *Beer: The Story of the Pint*. He wrote, "Medieval ale brewers never seem to have boiled their worts at all."

There is some indirect evidence of hopped beer in ninth-century Europe, but widespread use of hops in brewing before the twelfth century seems unlikely. The revolution of hopped beer began in the thirteenth century, but to my mind the truly revolutionary change involved not just hops—it involved boiling the wort with hops.

Ancient Fermentation

The first beers were made with spontaneous fermentation by wild yeast and bacteria residing in the surroundings, ingredients, and equipment. At some point, brewers began harvesting yeast from the fermenter and adding it to the next batch, thereby creating domesticated house yeasts. This domestication took place centuries before Louis Pasteur discovered the actual mechanism of fermentation in the nineteenth century, but we don't know exactly when.

Historian Richard W. Unger states in his book *Beer in the Middle Ages and the Renaissance* that brewers were already reusing yeast in the fourteenth century. Several written sources make it clear that yeast reuse was a common practice among both domestic brewers and larger-scale commercial brewers by the sixteenth century. In the article "Domestication and Divergence of *Saccharomyces cerevisiae* Beer Yeasts," a group of scientists analyzed the genomes of 157 industrial yeasts and estimated that some of the beer yeasts studied had been domesticated in the sixteenth century. However, there are several good reasons to believe that domestication of yeast began considerably earlier.

Spontaneous fermentation of beer typically leads to mixed fermentation by yeast and souring bacteria. This is a race of microbes. If souring bacteria seize the wort first, the acidity they produce can halt the alcoholic fermentation. Eventually, hardier yeast kicks in and ferments the beer, but that will take months, much as with Belgian lambics today. Likewise, if a yeast fit for producing higher levels of alcohol gets a head start, the bacteria will have difficulties in immediately producing high levels of acidity. In other words, spontaneous fermentation is a very slow and unpredictable way of getting more than a few percent alcohol. Likely very early on, the brewers of intoxicating feast ales had a more reliable method of fermentation. Perhaps unknowingly, they started to favor yeast over souring bacteria, which gave them at least a small window for drinking their ale before it went sour.

Some Norwegian and Lithuanian farmhouse brewers still harvest and store their heirloom house yeast with extremely simple yet effective methods. We don't know how old those yeasts and practices are, but the methods may have been practiced thousands of years ago—no special equipment or scientific know-how is required, just folk wisdom. Actually, some of these farmhouse yeasts are mixed cultures of yeast and bacteria, but in skilled hands they produce sweet and tasty ale that will become sour only by accident. The first written text on brewing sahti, from 1780, clearly states that the brewer adds house yeast and that she knows methods for avoiding sourness.

Norwegian beer writer Lars Marius Garshol has been a strong proponent of the idea that people were able to make tasty nonsour beer long before Pasteur's day. He has noted that several late medieval texts describe sour beer as undesired and mention tricks to avoid sourness in beer.

For example, Olaus Magnus's *Historia de Gentibus Septentrionalibus* (*History of the Northern Peoples*), published in 1555, mentions that beer should be sweet or bitter, and that winter is the best time to brew, because beer doesn't turn sour then. Magnus also says that beer is fermented with the dregs of the previous batch, or with bread yeast if the dregs are unavailable.

In addition, Martyn Cornell has uncovered several old English texts that contain similar evidence. In *Beer: The Story of the Pint*, he describes eleventh-century English writings that draw a distinction between "sweet ale" and "clear ale." It seems that sweet ale was meant to be consumed fresh, before it could go sour, while clear ale was kept longer and was allowed to sour. An English beer recipe dating from around 1430, found in a collection of writings known as the Paston Letters, has the line "And

Old sahti-drinking vessels at the Linen and Sahti Museum in Lammi. Clearly the ale was brewed and consumed in quantity.

nota that the ey of the henne shal kepe the ale fro sour," which in modern English reads as "Note that the hen's egg will keep the ale from going sour" (excerpt and translation from Cornell's *Zythophile* blog).

However, we cannot be sure what people of the past conceived of as "sour." Slightly acidic ale that we would now describe as sour or infected might not be sour by medieval standards.

People had a sweet tooth back in days of yore, too, but sources of sweetness were scarce, especially in northern Europe. In many areas, honey was difficult to obtain and a luxury of the privileged. Sugar was already known in medieval Europe, but it was an expensive flavoring then. It's likely that sweet ale was highly praised in the past, much as it is among the traditional brewers in the Nordic and Baltic countries today.

In conclusion, fermentation is undoubtedly the aspect of beer history we know the least about, and the earliest evidence of house yeast comes to us from the late Middle Ages. However, there is indirect evidence that yeast was domesticated much earlier, and it is entirely possible that the Norwegian and Lithuanian farmhouse yeasts are descended from yeasts of Viking times.

Finally, low-alcohol farmhouse ales are a completely different story. In parts of Finland, for example, some of the everyday ales were spontaneously fermented even within the last century. In those ales, fermentation was mostly a preservation method, and sour fermentation was part of the deal.

Iron Age Ale

Let's rewind to the Germanic tribes, Celts, and Vikings of the first millennium. How close were their ales to the Nordic and Baltic farmhouse ales brewed today? Direct evidence tells us mainly that those peoples all preferred to brew from malted barley and made beer in large quantities for their feasts.

The earliest written evidence of Germanic and Celtic brewing comes from Roman historians who regarded these northern neighbors as barbarians, as Max Nelson explains in his book *The Barbarian's Beverage: A History of Beer in Ancient Europe*. For example, around the first century AD, Tacitus described Germanic beer as "a liquid from barley or wheat, which, once rotted, has a certain resemblance to wine," as Nelson translated from the Latin. The Roman writings reveal little about the brewing techniques, but at least we know that the Germanic tribes and Celts had no difficulties in brewing large quantities of intoxicating ale.

Through the Viking sagas we know a little more about Viking ale. Neither recipes nor brewing processes were recorded, but the texts give insights to the role of ale in society. For example, several verses of *The Poetic Edda* advise drinking ale in moderation. Apparently, that didn't always happen. For the Vikings, ale was an important element of hospitality, and generous feasts showcased one's social status too. Extensive feasts were needed to establish alliances. The grandest feasts lasted several days, which is not that different from weddings of the twentieth century in the Nordic provinces renowned for their farmhouse ales. A German chronicler, Adam of Bremen, wrote around 1050 that Danish king Svein Estridsson held a sumptuous feast for eight successive days to confirm a treaty.

The Germanic people, Celts, and Vikings drank mead and wine also, which were highly regarded prestige drinks. These people lived largely outside grape-growing regions, and wine was an imported luxury product. Both mead and wine are often mentioned in the Viking sagas, because they were the most prestigious, but likely also the rarest of the feast drinks. No doubt the Vikings made mead themselves, but it seems that they usually had to import honey for it. A feast mead requires more than a pound of honey per gallon of drink (more than 1.2 kilograms for every 10 liters), so ale was probably a more typical feast drink. The Germans, Celts, and Vikings likely made weaker, low-alcohol ale in addition, for day-to-day consumption, but there is little evidence of this.

That the feasts featured ale in abundance is important as we dig into history, because it places constraints on the equipment and brewing techniques. Malting needed to be efficient and brewing vats large. The *Orkneyinga Saga* (the saga of the Orkney Islanders) states that large ale vats were placed near the entrance of the drinking hall. Hence, it was important also for there to be a functioning brewhouse nearby as the source for their contents, as Graham and Merryn Dineley pointed out in their article "Where Were the Viking Brew Houses?"

Staved wooden vats represented typical first-millennium technology and were the most practical large brewing vessels of the time. Large cauldrons or kettles were rare, so the Germanic tribes, Celts, and Vikings had to resort to farmhouse brewing techniques described earlier. They were probably not boiling their wort, and why would they? All the beer would get drunk before the feast was over anyway.

Because hops were not a typical ingredient in brews of the first millennium, juniper, bog myrtle, meadowsweet, and yarrow were more likely seasonings, and some brews may well have had no seasonings at all. Interestingly, there is some archaeological evidence that the Vikings grew hops in their gardens, but we don't know if it was for beer. In the past, hops have been grown for rope-making and dyeing as well. In areas where honey was available, it probably found its way into feast ales occasionally, as with gotlandsdricke today. The yeast and fermentation remain a big unknown.

Accordingly, the feast ales of the Germanic tribes, Celts, and Vikings in the first millennium were in many ways similar to present-day Nordic and Baltic farmhouse ales. Although these peoples are known for their warriors, most were farmers. In fact, in the first millennium the majority of northern Europeans lived on farms, and no doubt brewing was a common activity for them.

Brew like a Viking—the sahti brewery Olu Bryki Raum demonstrates historical brewing techniques at the Medieval Market of Turku, 2016. COURTESY OF SAMI BRODKIN

Apparently, the common origins of farmhouse ales like sahti, koduõlu, gotlandsdricke, maltøl, and kaimiškas were formed during the Iron Age, not later than the Viking Age. Obviously, the tiny amount of hops used in Nordic and Baltic farmhouse ales entered the tradition later on. Had Nordic and Baltic peoples adopted brewing after the Viking Age, they would have been making hopped beers brewed in line with more modern methods introduced in the late Middle Ages.

Medieval Ale

In the early Middle Ages, Europe was still the domain of unhopped ale. The transition to hopped beer came to Britain later than it did to continental Europe, and in the fourteenth century even the commercial ale in Britain was largely brewed with simple domestic techniques. Evidence of this shows up in tax logs, laws, and other written documents. Therefore, British beer history is a great source of information on preindustrial medieval brewing techniques.

Historian Judith Bennett describes these domestic brewing techniques in her book *Ale, Beer, and Brewsters in England*. For example, Bennett writes, "In 1333–34, the household of Elizabeth de Burgh, Lady of Clare, brewed about 8 quarters of barley and dredge each week, each quarter yielding about 60 gallons of ale."

Dredge refers to a combination of oats and barley, and a *quarter* is a unit of volume roughly equivalent to 77 US gallons (290 liters). The weight of a quarter of malt is in the range of 250–340 pounds (113–154 kilograms), depending on the malt type and malting techniques. Finally, 60 imperial gallons is equivalent to 72 US gallons (273 liters). Thus, approximately 1 pound of grain was used to brew 1 quart of ale (1 kilogram of grain was used for every 2 liters of ale). This ratio is similar to that used for sahti.

At the time of Elizabeth de Burgh, stronger ale was brewed from the undiluted first wort, and then the mash was rinsed with water to make a weaker ale from the late runnings. Even if one assumes very low malt-sugar extraction, the first wort could have easily been of 18°P gravity, capable of fermenting to around 7 percent ABV. However, this example comes from a household of the nobility, able to afford stronger ale. Malt quantities in poorer households could have been half of de Burgh's.

According to Bennett, the fourteenth-century English ale was made from an unboiled wort. The brewsters might have had cauldrons for heating water, but bigger vessels suitable for boiling the wort were rare. Although sometimes the brew was flavored with herbs gathered in the wild, often the ingredients were simply water, malt, and yeast. Most of these ales were meant to be consumed very fresh, but evidently the Anglo-Saxons also had some kind of stock ale that could withstand storage.

On the continent, the most renowned brew before hopped beer was so-called *gruit ale*, brewed roughly where northern Germany, the Netherlands, and Belgium are today. Starting in around the ninth or tenth century, this ale was brewed for centuries with a highly regulated and taxed herb mixture called *gruit*. Its composition was often kept secret, but bog myrtle is commonly believed to have been the most important constituent.

Not much is known about the brewing process for gruit ales, but probably it was similar to that used with medieval British ales, except for the herbal mixture. Most gruit ales likely were raw ales consumed when fresh. Though there are similarities, unhopped British ales or Nordic farmhouse ales shouldn't be regarded as examples of historical gruit ales—true gruit ales were highly regulated with an herb monopoly beyond the control of brewers.

In England domestic brewers were outdone by competing large-scale producers of hopped beer by the seventeenth century. Archaic unhopped ales disappeared from the market, although they continued to be brewed for countryside households into the eighteenth century.

On the continent, both the decline of domestic ales and the triumph of hopped beers occurred much earlier. It is commonly accepted that the scaling up and development of brewing techniques in Europe began in monasteries around the eighth to ninth century. The monasteries needed large amounts of beer for the staff and visitors, and they also had surplus time and wealth for these developments. Gradually, commercial breweries caught up with advances in technology, which required more capital but were more efficient. The more efficient brewers were using cultivated hops instead of mostly wild-grown brewing herbs. This eventually pushed hopped beers into the mainstream and unhopped ales onto the sidelines.

In conclusion, it seems that many sahti-like features were typical of the pre-hop medieval ales, even at urban commercial breweries. They were typically raw ales for immediate consumption. Medieval ales were unlike sahti in one respect, however: they were more often part of the daily diet and not restricted to feasts.

Reenactors drinking sahti at the Medieval Market of Turku in 2018. COURTESY OF SAMI BRODKIN

The History of Sahti in Finland

Before the thirteenth century, what is now Finland was the domain of various tribes, and history wasn't written down. From around the thirteenth century to 1809, most of Finland belonged to the Kingdom of Sweden, and beer appears in official documents from the fourteenth century onward. With Swedish rule came officials, noblemen, merchants, and craftsmen from Sweden and Germany, who brought a thirst for the beer they had been used to in their homelands—likely to have been hopped beer à la northern Germany. At first, beer was imported to Finland, but gradually local hop farming and brewing were built up.

Accordingly, the beer drunk in the cities and at castles and manors was hopped and brewed in accordance with continental methods. That beer was made in several strengths, but in general it was weak and consumed daily in large quantities. The lower one's rank and social status, the lower the alcohol content of the beer. Old written sources make it clear also that the farming folk had their own ale, but the nature of these domestic ales wasn't recorded until the first ethnographic study by Hellenius was printed, in 1780.

Finnish ethnographers mapped the areas of living farmhouse brewing traditions around 1900, at which time around 90 percent of Finns still lived in the countryside. The surveys give a good idea of the extent of the culture at that time, and likely centuries before. Sahti was widely brewed in western Finland, and in the north the traditions extended almost to the limits of cultivation. Today the areas of this traditional living culture have shrunk to about forty municipalities.

Historically, Finland has been at an intersection of western and eastern cultures, and this is apparent in the farmhouse brewing traditions. Sahti is clearly a tradition of western Finland, and it seems related to Scandinavian and Germanic brewing. Through the ages, western Finland has received Scandinavian immigrants, and even today the Finns in the west are genetically closer to Swedes than to people in eastern Finland.

In eastern Finland, in essence the area east of the sahti districts, farmers made low-alcohol ales surprisingly different from sahti. I will elaborate on the contrast between western and eastern farmhouse brewing in the chapter "Low-Alcohol Farmhouse Ales" (page 95).

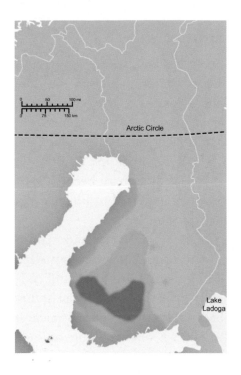

The areas where traditions of sahti-style brewing remained at the dawn of the twentieth century, according to ethnographer Matti Räsänen. The current heartland of sahti is in darker shades. The large diagonal break in this area is known as the Suomenselkä ridge and consists of infertile land that apparently is not the best area for self-sufficient brewing. The areas near Lake Ladoga were part of Finnish territory until they were lost to the Soviet Union in the Second World War. MIKA LAITINEN

The ethnographic map of sahti traditions in about 1900 also shows a few odd isolated spots in eastern Finland that do not follow expected patterns. Ethnographer Matti Räsänen, who analyzed the surveys' results, mentioned that brewing was not very common there. The spots around Lake Ladoga are particularly interesting. Did this area's traditions carry over from the Viking Age, when the Vikings traveled east via Lake Ladoga?

Sahti in the Modern Era

The sixteenth century saw distillation spread to Finland, which definitely changed the society's customs and attitudes toward drinking. In some areas, distilled alcohol came to rival beer as a feast drink and sign of hospitality. In 1866 home distillation became illegal, but homebrewing for one's own consumption remained an important civil right until prohibition arrived in the twentieth century.

The farm folk made a clear distinction between sahti and distilled alcohol, and they generally believed that these drinks lead to different kinds of drunkenness. In folklore, a sahti drinker becomes drowsy and jovial, while spirits may arouse anger. These beliefs have been immortalized in several sayings, such as "he wasn't drunk; he had been drinking sahti."

In Finland the temperance movement began to gain traction near the end of the nineteenth century, and full prohibition entered force in 1919. This brought ruin to the brewing industry, and in urban areas beer was replaced with smuggled booze. Prohibition was repealed in 1932, but alcohol in Finland has remained highly regulated ever since. Officially, prohibition did extend to sahti, but the people of the farmhouses remained loyal to their ale traditions, and brewing of sahti was tacitly

The *Kalevala*, the national epic of Finland, explains the creation of the world and the origins of beer, among other things. While a fascinating piece of mythology and folklore, it is very problematic as a historical reference. It was compiled in the nineteenth century by Elias Lönnrot on the basis of Finnish folklore of several eras. Some of the runes may be thousands of years old, but putting a date to them is next to impossible. Furthermore, Lönnrot wrote some of the material himself, to stitch together a consistent story. This classic illustration for the epic was painted by Akseli Gallen-Kallela. TURKU ART MUSEUM, COURTESY OF WIKIMEDIA COMMONS

accepted by the local authorities. In the heyday of the temperance movement, some social customs formerly associated with beer shifted to coffee,
and today Finns drink the most coffee per capita in the world.

In the late nineteenth century, sahti was still brewed self-sufficiently.
The twentieth century brought significant changes, as farmers switched
to commercial baker's yeast and malt, but in most cases the brewing process remained archaic and true to the family traditions.

In the 1980s, the idea of commercial sahti took hold in several heartland counties. The first commercial brewer of sahti to begin operations
was Lammin Sahti, in 1987, and a few others quickly followed. These
commercial breweries were small-scale, but they opened the eyes of a
larger audience and helped to preserve the tradition. In 2002 sahti was
granted the European Union's "Traditional Speciality Guaranteed" appellation, which defines what is considered authentic commercial sahti.

Beer writer Michael Jackson had mentioned sahti already in 1977 in his
legendary *The World Guide to Beer*, and through his writings sahti became
internationally known as one of the oldest and most unusual beer styles.
He visited Finland several times, meeting both commercial and domestic
brewers. Even today, international pilgrims show up in the rural municipality of Lammi, largely because Michael Jackson enjoyed sahti there.

In the 1990s, Jackson visited farmhouse breweries in Norway, Gotland, Estonia, Latvia, and Lithuania also, but he wrote the most about
sahti. I find this mysterious. After all, his grandparents were Lithuanian.
Perhaps he wanted to write about the brews that were reasonably available, or maybe it had to do with the holy combination of sauna and sahti,
on which Jackson commented in his witty style, "I have on more than one
occasion suffered the heat, steam, smoke and birching in the sauna, and
the cold water of the lake, to drink this beer."

Etymology

Across the Nordic and Baltic countries, the word for beer has the same—
presumably Germanic—origin as *ale*: *olut* in Finland, *õlu* in Estonia, *öl* in
Sweden, *øl* in Denmark and Norway, *alus* in Lithuania and Latvia. Also,
in the British Isles the word *ale* used to refer to beer in general, until in
the late Middle Ages when its meaning was restricted to unhopped beer,
before convoluting to its current meaning of top-fermenting beer.

In the old days, when countryside folk drank only their own beer, the drink we today call sahti was known as *olut*, *olu*, or *olvi*. Usually *olut* wasn't used for just any beer; the word was reserved for the farmhouse's best beer, not to be confused with ordinary low-alcohol ale. Often the daily low-alcohol ale was called *kalja* in Finland and *kali* in Estonia.

The etymology of *sahti* is peculiar, and it seems that the word came to be attached to farmhouse beer only in the last few centuries. As far as I know, similar words for beer don't exist in any other countries or languages. For example, the farmhouse beer in Estonia is still known as *koduõlu*, translating as "homemade beer."

The most plausible explanation is that *sahti* comes from the Swedish word *saft*, which is derived, in turn, from the Germanic *saf*, meaning "juice" or "sap." From old Finnish dictionaries of the 1700s and 1800s, it seems that originally *sahti* referred to low-alcohol beer made from the late runnings. Often the late-runnings ales were only slightly fermented, something like soft drinks of their day, so this explanation makes sense. In Finnish folklore, beer has been called "milk of the fields" also, and the poetic expression "juice of grain" doesn't sound far off in this respect.

Around the late nineteenth and early twentieth century, *sahti* gained popularity as a synonym for *olut*. Then, as industrial beer became widely available in the countryside in the first half of the twentieth century, a distinction was drawn: *sahti* shifted in meaning, to refer to homemade beer, while *olut* came to be associated with industrial beer.

Nobody can explain how this Swedish word drifted into the vocabulary of Finnish-speaking farmers, but the Finnish language in general has plenty of loan words from Swedish. An unproven theory claims that people began to refer to farmhouse ale as "juice" to mislead the Swedish-speaking taxmen.

Finnish and Estonian are Finno-Ugric languages and linguistically very distant from Germanic languages such as English, German, Swedish, Danish, and Norwegian. Yet the brewing vocabulary used for sahti and for koduõlu have mostly Germanic origins. Consider these Finnish words: *mallas* ("malt," cognate to German *Malz*), *mäski* ("mash," from the German *Maische*), and *vierre* ("wort," from the German *Würze*).

Hence, the etymology of brewing-related words is another factor suggesting that sahti and koduõlu, along with other northern farmhouse ales, have been handed down from an ancient Germanic tradition of brewing.

— 5 —

Drinking Sahti

Is It a Beer Style?

S AHTI HAS SURVIVED the arrival of distilled alcohol, the onset of the
era of cheap industrial beer, and prohibition. Without its rich and
unique taste, the tradition would surely have been dead by now. I will
now put that "rich and unique" properly into words, describing what
makes a genuine sahti and what is considered inauthentic. Since sahti is
essentially a tradition of homebrewing, I will be speaking more from a
domestic perspective.

Farmhouse ales always pose a challenge for those who want to cate-
gorize beers by style. Brewer-specific variation is enormous, and regional
preferences may be overshadowed by "noisy" individual examples. In
addition, with freshly consumed farmhouse ales such as sahti, the age
of the ale plays an important role. The ale can even taste different on the
same day, depending on whether the pint was drawn from the top or the
bottom of the fermenter.

Nevertheless, sahti enthusiasts are highly opinionated about what
makes proper sahti. Inevitably, matters related to a beer style are woven
into time and space, and drinkers base their understanding on their palate. Today's conceptions may not cover truly historical versions crafted
from smoky homemade malt and fermented at milk-warm temperatures
with house yeast.

At the two extremes of debate, I have seen narrow style guidelines
that would exclude most Finnish sahtis and heard arguments that sahti

Sahti is often described as noncarbonated, but a pour straight from the brewer's cellar
can be lively. Whenever someone tries to classify homemade farmhouse ales, there will
be plenty of exceptions.

The color range of sahti is wide, but in many traditional districts reddish brown is the norm.

isn't a beer style at all. I do think that sahti can be called a beer style, but the guidelines applied need to be very broad.

Appearance

Generally the color of sahti varies from yellow to dark brown, but a reddish-brown hue is the most appreciated. The color is surprisingly important to sahti folks, and the mere appearance can provoke strong prejudices surrounding how the drink will taste. Once when I served a straw-colored sahti in Finland's National Sahti Competition, a lady commented that "it looks like urine." I had to cajole her to taste it, and after a distrustful sip she noted, "Not bad."

Sahtis in shades of yellow or orange are still made in a few municipalities, but further from home they are usually frowned upon. That's a pity, because lighter malt can express refreshing summery qualities of cereals that are absent from heartier and breadier darker ales. A hazy light-colored appearance can give the impression of yeastiness, perhaps the root of the prejudices.

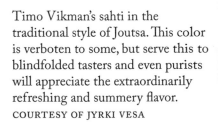

Timo Vikman's sahti in the traditional style of Joutsa. This color is verboten to some, but serve this to blindfolded tasters and even purists will appreciate the extraordinarily refreshing and summery flavor.
COURTESY OF JYRKI VESA

Sahti is typically hazy, but that is due more to proteins in the wort than yeast. A small amount of yeast is usually suspended in the liquid and can even add to the taste, but an obvious sensation of yeastiness is considered a flaw. Sometimes a few weeks of cool storage can render the ale almost bright, but crystal-clear appearance prompts the question "Is that really traditionally brewed?"

Carbonation

In the old days, sahti was transferred to a wooden cask as soon as the most vigorous fermentation had calmed down. The cask was sealed gently to prevent bursting but still allow some pressure buildup. Old tales describe sahti "kicking" in the cask, and several stories praise the pleasures of a fresh frothy sahti. The first pours may well have been lively and foamy. As more ale was drawn, the liveliness was lost, and the sahti became gradually more still, much like a cask-conditioned ale does.

Today sahti is usually served still, but some brewers prefer a gentle fizz created by sluggish secondary fermentation in the storage vessel. Even if the fizz is hardly visible, it can add to the mouthfeel. Hence, whether we consider historical or contemporary sahti, both still and smoothly carbonated from residual fermentation are authentic. Priming with sugar or injecting carbon dioxide would certainly be considered untraditional among Finns.

Elsewhere in the Nordic and Baltic countries, still or nearly still farmhouse ales are certainly common, but I have encountered more relaxed attitudes toward carbonation too. In Lithuania and Norway, I've enjoyed frothy pints of otherwise very traditional farmhouse ales, force-carbonated from a stainless steel keg. In Estonia koduõlu is often kept in locally welded stainless steel kegs that can withstand high pressure, and the residual fermentation can yield very frothy first pours. This actually happened to a friend of mine: guy walks into a bar in Saaremaa and orders a koduõlu. The bartender tries to pour a pint, but it is all foam. Luckily he knows a cunning farmhouse trick: he takes a pinch of butter into his fingers and greases the pint glass to suppress excessive foaming.

Some people clearly prefer their farmhouse ale at least slightly carbonated. To my mind, full-bodied sahti is perfectly fine served still, but farmhouse ales with lighter texture benefit from smooth carbonation.

Strength and Body

Being a premium celebration ale, sahti is expected to be satisfying and intoxicating. The malt-sugar content, or gravity, should be so high that even after production of a considerable amount of alcohol, plenty of residual malt sugars remain to contribute to mouthfeel and nourishment.

The mouthfeel and body are further enhanced by a generous amount of proteins, which are not precipitated by an hour-long wort boil. Add to this rye with its oily viscous compounds (beta glucans), and you have a thick milkshake-like texture.

Despite the strength, sahti is not a sipping beer. At celebrations it is consumed in pints, and well-made sahti is deceptively drinkable. Seasoned drinkers have a humble respect for the strength and know their limits, while others have cause to be really wary.

In 2014 the scientists of VTT Technical Research Centre of Finland analyzed twelve sahtis entered in the National Sahti Competition and published the results in the *Journal of the Institute of Brewing*. The samples were randomly selected from among entries by forty-nine competitors, from all traditional sahti districts. The selection was evenly distributed

According to an old saying, "In drinking sahti, the feet get drunk first, and then the head." Many can attest to this from personal experience. My theory is that the high sugar content invigorates the mind so much that the first sign of intoxication is a lack of coordination. Indeed, with plenty of residual malt sugars and its nutrients, sahti is akin to a sports drink with alcohol in it. Devilish drinkability certainly plays a role in the sudden inebriation too.

geographically, and in my view it was a representative sample of home-made sahtis.

On average, these twelve sahtis had 7.9 percent ABV. Ten samples featured an alcohol content above 7 percent, and the strongest was 10.5 percent. Two sahtis stood out for their comparatively low alcohol content: 3.7 and 5 percent.

The scientists measured residual extract also, on the Plato scale (°P). On average, the residual extract level was 9.5°P, and several samples had levels of 11 to 12°P. This means that the amount of malt sugars remaining in most of these sahtis is what typical 4 to 5 percent commercial beers have before fermentation! The two lower-alcohol sahtis were extremely high in residual extract (at 18.2°P and 12.3°P); this shows that they were underfermented rather than low in gravity. From the alcohol content and the residual extract, the researchers estimated that the starting gravities must have been very high, around 25°P on average.

Aroma and Flavor

Substantial fresh maltiness is expected of sahti, and that typically comes with aromas and flavors of bread, toffee, and honey. Especially in a raw ale, the flavor emerges with fresh cereals, unlike in any modern beer. Sahti need not contain rye, but often dark rye malt is included, bringing qualities of rye bread, toasted nuts, and chocolate.

Rustic fruity and spicy flavors from the fermentation are an important characteristic too. Depending on brewer preferences, fruitiness and spiciness may rival the maltiness, but fermentation-related character can be subdued, leaving center stage to the malt. Most brewers use the same brand of Finnish baker's yeast, which typically manifests itself in flavors of banana and clove, somewhat similar to Bavarian wheat-beer (*weizen*) yeast. Sahti is often noted as having bananas in the aroma, but this is by no means a requirement. Alcohol warmth can be a pleasant promise of strength, but solventy or boozy notes are not valued.

Most brewers use juniper branches at some point in the process, but they generally aim for a smooth and restrained taste. In fact, I have never heard people complain about lack of juniper flavor, even though some brewers make fine sahti without any juniper whatsoever. There is no hop character to speak of, and counting bitterness units is irrelevant.

Koduõlu, the Estonian cousin of sahti, is typically straw-colored, often with opaque haze. In both appearance and flavor, it bears a close resemblance to a light-colored sahti, such as that of Joutsa. Homemade koduõlu is often served in a traditional tankard, typically made from juniper or pine. The perfumed coniferous scent imparted by the wood is part of the experience.

It is often stated that beer needs some kind of bittering agent to counterbalance the sweet maltiness. In the case of boiled-wort beer, I'm inclined to agree (perhaps if excluding sour ales), but brewing raw ales is a different game. Proteins and all those things that don't precipitate out in the boil make these ales less sweet, and a raw ale without any seasonings can be perfectly balanced. Besides, rustic fermentation adds quite a bit of counterbalance in its own right. Admittedly, sahti is typically quite sweet, and folks like it that way.

Sourness is something sahti people despise, and brewers generally try to avoid it. However, sourness may sneak in slowly: before becoming clearly sour, sahti may take on acceptable or even pleasant tartness. Even the best sahtis may eventually turn sour, but that is merely a sign that the drink is too old or has been improperly stored.

VTT's analysis of twelve sahtis revealed interesting fermentation characteristics. Isoamyl acetate, the main chemical compound behind banana aromas, measured high in ten of the sahtis. The same ten samples had high levels of 4-vinyl guaiacol, which manifests itself in beer as clovey spiciness. In fact, these ten samples had more of both of these compounds than two commercial Bavarian weizens chosen as reference beers, and several of the sahtis had double or threefold this concentration, even though weizens in particular are known for their aromas of banana and clove!

The two outliers that were low in alcohol were remarkably different in fermentation characteristics. They measured low in both isoamyl acetate and 4-vinyl guaiacol. Also, they were low in pH (3.95 and 4.2) and high in both lactic and acetic acid. Clearly, souring bacteria were emerging, but high sweetness may have masked the sour taste. Without tasting the samples and interviewing the brewers, one cannot say whether these two sahtis were what the brewers intended. The other ten samples had a pH above 4.3 and showed no symptoms of sourness.

The Geography of Sahti

As we saw in the chapter "History of Farmhouse Ales," in roughly 1900 the whole of western Finland, apart from some nonarable land, was home to sahti. Since then, the areas where these traditions thrive have shrunk to around forty municipalities, and now sahti is a regional specialty, confined mainly to the sparsely populated countryside of Finland. The number of

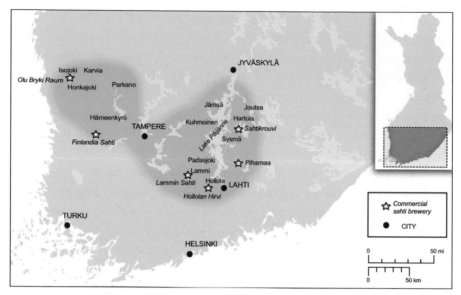

The regions where there are living sahti traditions. This map shows the municipalities most renowned for their sahti, and the six commercial sahti breweries. The cities of Lahti and Tampere, lying in the heart of sahti territory, have plenty of brewers too, but the traditions have become mixed on account of the influx of people from neighboring regions. A new generation of brewers has revived the tradition in many areas—for example, around Helsinki. MIKA LAITINEN

brewers is unknown, but it is probably in the range of five hundred to one thousand.

Sahti shows geographical variation and even regional substyles, but the distinctions are blurred somewhat by enormous brewer-to-brewer variation—even neighbors can make surprisingly different sahti. For this reason, the geographical differences are unclear to many, although sahti folks like to contrast themselves to those in the next district over.

Ask a Finn to name notable sahti districts, and the small countryside municipality of Lammi will probably get mentioned first. This is home to the best-known commercial sahti brewer, Lammin Sahti, and to its founder, Pekka Kääriäinen, the most vocal Finnish spokesman for the tradition. It was in Lammi that esteemed beer writer Michael Jackson penned his most quoted praises of sahti. The local sahti here is reddish brown and sweet, with a fair amount of dark rye malt (around 10 percent) and a distinct aroma of banana. This is in line with the typical image of sahti.

Lammi and its surroundings form a haven for particularly sweet and dark sahti. The tendency is especially apparent in the nearby municipality of Padasjoki, 20 miles (30 kilometers) north of Lammi. Padasjoki has plenty of active brewers who faithfully follow family traditions, and in a surprisingly similar style. These sahtis are among the darkest, with generous use of dark rye malt giving a distinctive taste of rye-bread crust. To counterbalance the toasty notes, these brewers make their sahti sweet and full-bodied. The brewers generally prefer slower fermentation at colder temperatures, which makes for a very malt-forward sahti.

Another hotspot of sweet and dark sahti is Hämeenkyrö, 80 miles (130 kilometers) west of Padasjoki, although these municipalities are not geographically connected. The locals in Hämeenkyrö are very proud of their brewing traditions and of award-winning masters of it, among them Olavi Viheroja, two-times winner of the National Sahti Competition. The coat of arms of Hämeenkyrö even features a drinking horn.

Lake Päijänne is a fairly large body of water almost completely surrounded by countryside municipalities where sahti is an integral part of life. The "sweet and dark" districts, such as Lammi and Padasjoki, are south and southwest of the lake. The area to the east of Lake Päijänne has a brewing culture all its own, especially clustered around the municipalities of Sysmä, Hartola, and Joutsa.

Eastward of Lake Päijänne, rye malt plays a smaller role, and some brewers make sahti from barley alone. Many brewers like to leave out the dark rye malt, thus creating a mellower ale without toasted notes. Some brewers darken their ales with caramel barley malt, but others are satisfied with a yellow-orange color. Some of the paler versions are lower in alcohol and lighter in body too.

Another distinct eastern feature is more expressive fermentation, with pronounced fruitiness and tartness. Those in the sweet-and-dark camp sometimes claim that sahtis on the eastern side of Lake Päijänne are sour, which is almost an insult to a brewer. I find this claim to be a misconception, and perhaps stemming from badmouthing between rival districts. Some eastern versions have a pleasant, refreshing tartness, but I would not call them sour.

A third distinctive branch of the tradition is rye sahti, which is made especially around the municipalities of Isojoki and Honkajoki, in western Finland. Farmers in these regions have favored growing rye, and plenty of it has ended up in sahti too, in both malted and unmalted form. Today in Isojoki and Honkajoki, pale rye malt typically fills 25 to 40 percent of the malt bill, with a touch of dark rye malt added for color. Because rye has a fairly bold taste, this kind of sahti certainly stands out. Generally, these sahtis are less sweet, and the flavor is centered on malt and cereal, with grainy and nutty flavors of rye.

Although I maintain that there are three major subcategories of sahti, other districts have their local characteristics too, but with more subtle distinctions. For this brief survey of the geography of sahti, of necessity I have left out many active and tradition-rich districts with fine brewers.

The "Traditional Speciality Guaranteed" Appellation

In 2002 sahti was granted the Traditional Speciality Guaranteed (TSG) appellation of the European Union, which regulates what can be sold as sahti within the European Union. The specification does not limit where sahti is made, only how it is produced. For example, most Estonian koduõlus would meet the requirements and could be sold as sahti.

Accordingly, it does not directly concern homebrewers as such. Nevertheless, it is the foremost specification of what is authentic sahti, so homebrewers refer to it if the authenticity is questioned. The main definition connected with the TSG appellation reads thus:

> Sahti is traditionally prepared from raw materials including, in addition to malted barley, other cereal malt and cereals (rye, barley, wheat and oats) and usually hops, fermented using baker's yeast or harvested yeast.

The application documents on the webpages of the EU contain a few additional specifications. For example, the original gravity of sahti should be at least 19°P, and the alcohol content should be 6 to 12 percent by volume. The contribution to this gravity should come only from malted and unmalted grains. Obviously, sahti should be unfiltered and unpasteurized. Somewhat surprisingly, juniper is mentioned only as a filtering aid, not as an ingredient.

The description is kept short in the interest of easy regulation, so it does not cover all the geographical and historical variations. As the study by VTT showed, not all homebrewed versions comply with the alcohol requirement associated with the appellation. Surely many true farmhouse sahtis of the past wouldn't meet the guidelines either. Therefore, homebrewers should look at the specification with common sense, reflecting on the ingredients and brewing process in light of the old farmhouse traditions.

As the main advocate of the appellation, Pekka Kääriäinen stresses that genuine sahti can be made with ingredients and methods not mentioned in the appellation, so long as they are justifiably traditional. The appellation should only prevent misrepresentation of the tradition, not restrict it. By 2018 two beers sold in Finland have been deemed to breach the appellation's terms: one was fermented with brewer's yeast, and the other was too low in alcohol.

The National Sahti Competition

The yearly National Sahti Competition event for homebrewers was established in 1992 to preserve the tradition. It is an important showcase for the diversity of sahti, and it draws hundreds of brewers and drinkers from all the major sahti districts. Simultaneously, comparing sahtis across

The National Sahti Competition has as many judges as there are competitors.

The parking lot at the National Sahti Competition is the best place to sample sahtis from all around Finland. An open trunk is the code for free samples. In principle, you could taste sahtis from all the major municipalities, but in practice you really need to watch your feet after twenty. COURTESY OF JYRKI VESA

regions has raised concerns: Are brewers tuning their traditional family recipes to win the competition? Might diversity ultimately be lost?

In parallel with the official program, there is an unofficial gathering, held in the parking lot. Brewers compare ales with each other and offer free samples for those in attendance. Some might serve extremely interesting brews that are too exuberant for the competition. Most likely, I'd be there too, chatting with brewers, trying various sahtis, and pouring samples of my own farmhouse brews.

The rules allow one competitor per municipality, making the event as much rivalry between municipalities as between brewers. Each competitor at the national level gets there by winning a local competition, which is no mean feat in hotspots of sahti. The number of competitors (or municipalities) used to be thirty to forty, but in the 2010s the total has risen to around fifty. The new municipalities are represented by city people who either have their roots in the sahti heartland or have caught the brewing bug elsewhere.

The competition has quite an original rule for making sure that the jury is geographically representative: each competitor brings his or her own judge. Traditionally the chairman, Pekka Kääriäinen, opens the competition with the words "all may favor their own municipality as much as they please," knowing that identifying the sahti from one's own municipality in blind judging is virtually impossible.

This peculiar judging system certainly affects what kinds of brews win and what gets brought in. Even if judges cannot identify their "home" competitor, they certainly notice the brews distinct from their local style. Often, samples that clearly stand out are eliminated first, such as paler sahtis. Nevertheless, most competitors swear that for the competition they brew as they always do. Some with a more competitive nature may fine-tune their brew to please the judges. There are those who bring in competition-geared sahti but then serve a family-style ale in the parking lot.

Storage and Shelf Life

I'm often asked what the fuss is about the short shelf life of sahti. Why is it so difficult to export? Why should sahti be kept cold while being transported? Could you brew it differently so that it would keep longer? Let me first explain why sahti needs to be stored so carefully and why it is best consumed soon after brewing.

Baker's yeast can contain small amounts of lactic bacteria. While this is not an issue in baking, the bugs can turn farmhouse ale sour if given a chance. I'm convinced that sahti going sour has to do mainly with baker's yeast, not the unboiled wort. I have brewed many raw ales with conventional brewer's yeast, and none of them have turned sour, even if stored at room temperature. Also, some farmhouse ales brewed with house yeasts are less sensitive to warm storage than sahti brewed with fresh Finnish baker's yeast.

Folk wisdom attests that fine, sweet, nonsour ale can be brewed even in the presence of souring bacteria, if the ale is kept warm only during the most vigorous fermentation. Continuous storage at cooler temperatures after fermentation is a traditional method of combating souring of beer, and this precaution is definitely needed with sahti.

Storage temperatures below 47°F (8°C) would be best, and 54°F (12°C) is passable to keep the drink safe for a week or two. Sometimes merely half a day at ambient temperature can kick off souring.

A wooden haarikka is the most traditional vessel for serving sahti. It is meant to be shared among drinkers, and usually it holds 5 or 6 pints. MIKA LAITINEN

The constraint of continuous cold storage makes traveling with sahti challenging, and even some experienced brewers have ruined their sahtis by transporting them in conditions that are too warm. I once took sahti from my home in central Finland to Copenhagen, a journey of 12 hours from fridge to fridge, and served it there in good condition. For longer travels I would freeze the sahti. This keeps it cool for a long time, but it would probably be best enjoyed within a few days after becoming liquid again.

The use of unboiled wort does cause the ale to get stale sooner, and since outstanding freshness is a hallmark of sahti, staleness in the taste is a critical flaw. Cold storage will not only prevent or slow down souring but also delay staling. With storage below 45°F (7°C), the shelf life of sahti can be as long as two or three months. Nevertheless, it is best to do as was traditionally done: aim the brew for a specific party, and consume the bulk of the ale there.

Alongside temperature and time, another factor in staling is the storage containers. Often sahti brewers store their ale in big plastic canisters, from which some of the ale is decanted for consumption. Obviously, ale sharing space with air in half-full containers will speed up the staling process, but using these containers will work for a few days, even weeks.

Most drinkers don't care for aged sahti, but forgotten bottles may actually develop pleasant vinous acidity with age—that is, for someone who enjoys sour ales. After a year or two in the cellar, some of my sahtis have emerged surprisingly similar to brown beers of Flanders, such as Liefmans Goudenband.

Serving Sahti

The most traditional way of serving sahti is from a wooden haarikka, which is intended to be passed around by the group. Sharing a drink with an honored guest or a friend is an age-old ritual, and I have been welcomed this way several times on my Nordic and Baltic travels. In Estonia I was passed a large wooden tankard of koduõlu, and in Norway six men drained a big wooden bowl of maltøl. Today haarikkas are not completely a thing of the past, but glassware of various kinds is far more typical. Sahti being a folk ale, serving methods tend to be uncomplicated and varied.

Farmhouse ale really blossoms in a tulip-shaped beer or wine glass, although this is not the most typical presentation.

In the old days, cold sahti was fetched from a cask with the haarikka or a bucket. The first sips were cellar-cold, and likely the last sips were considerably warmer. Still today, many serve their sahti straight from the cold storage area, without rushing to knock back the ale before it warms up. Some brewers argue that well-made sahti tastes good both cold and warm. Packed with taste, sahti doesn't lack character even if served fridge-cold. When warm, it tastes like a different ale but can be equally enjoyable.

Today most drinkers like their sahti cool, but some sahti folks actually prefer room temperature. I think this variation not only reflects personal tastes but also depends on the particular ale. Drier malt-forward sahti may be quite palatable warm, while some sweeter versions can become cloying. Also, highly fruity and spicy examples may taste too pungent above cellar temperatures. One peculiar old habit is to heat sahti to slightly

Sahti brewery and restaurant Hollolan Hirvi makes a dish that pairs perfectly with the sahti of the house: moose marinated in sahti, served with root vegetables and barley.

above body temperature—men working the whole day out in the cold have sometimes invigorated themselves with a pint of warmed-up sahti.

All that being said, a standard beer glass and a temperature range of 43–54°F (6–12°C) is always a safe bet. Note also that often the storage containers have plenty of sediment at the bottom, and pouring in the dregs should be avoided.

Since sahti is a celebration ale, it is often enjoyed with food, and it pairs extremely well with some traditional Finnish foods. Although sahti is wholesome nourishment by itself, it is often matched with hearty foods. In the lake districts, a perfect accompaniment is a whitefish known as vendace, fried crisp in butter. Smoke-cured ham or smoked fish (usually salmon) is another typical companion. Obviously, sahti and sandwiches made with rye bread are a perfect match. Pair sahti with Danish *smørrebrød* (an open-faced sandwich), and you have reached the heart of Nordic tastes. A more modern but equally delicious pairing is sweet farmhouse ale with salty cheese, such as blue cheese or old Gouda.

– 6 –

Commercial Production

Like Homemade?

THE LOCALS IN THE HEART OF SAHTI COUNTRY keep themselves
well stocked with homemade ale, but promoting the culture is difficult without a sellable product. This was the idea that led to commercial
exploitation of sahti in the 1980s, with the first licenses being granted for
commercial production in 1987. Since then, sahti has been a special feature at many Finnish summer events such as beer festivals and medieval
fairs. Both nationally and internationally, commercial sahti has provided
access to a culture that is noncommercial at its core.

While that first license in 1987 marked the beginnings of greater
prominence for sahti, there were actually commercial operations earlier: a
few brewers were selling sahti wort years before licenses for alcohol production were granted. Wort is a foodstuff and not subject to alcohol tax.
The downside is that the customers are the ones who ferment the wort,
and they don't always apply the same skill as the brewer. In this land of
extremely high alcohol taxes, the wort sold very well in the 1980s. For
example, sahti brewery Sahtikrouvi, which is still in operation, sold 8,000
gallons (30,000 liters) of wort annually during these peak years. Some
brewers still sell sahti wort, but demand is low today.

The first commercial brewery on the sahti scene was Lammin Sahti,
founded by Pekka and Sirpa Kääriäinen. It is still the biggest and most
renowned. In fact, Lammin Sahti boasts the oldest operational micro-
brewery in Finland. Cofounder Pekka Kääriäinen can be rightly called

Lammin Sahti is the first and still the best-known producer of commercial sahti. Lately,
they have begun to sell their ale in a pouch.

Pekka Kääriäinen, who has made more than a million liters of sahti, has been the most vocal of spokesmen for the tradition, alongside Michael Jackson.
COURTESY OF JYRKI VESA

Mr. Sahti, for acting as the driving force behind the TSG appellation, the National Sahti Competition, and many other sahti-related endeavors.

Fast-forwarding to 2018, we find six commercial breweries that specialize in sahti. Sahti is their flagship product, yet these are actually sideline operations or not so much a business as efforts to promote the tradition. The sahti breweries are shown on the map on page 66. In addition, various Finnish craft breweries make sahti occasionally, often as a special seasonal or single-festival brew.

Is It Like Homemade?

The question of authenticity always arises when a traditional homemade food or drink becomes a commercial product, and sahti is no exception. The producers need to earn the public's trust, and the consumers need to understand what makes an authentic product.

Pekka Kääriäinen assures that he brews Lammin Sahti just as he would at home, in the tradition of his home district, Lammi. The traditional brewing process can be fairly easily reproduced on larger scale, and the limitations related to cold storage and shelf life apply to commercial and home-based brewers alike. According to Kääriäinen, the main difference between homemade and commercial sahti involves how consistent the results are. The most widely available examples—Lammin Sahti and Finlandia Sahti—usually taste the same from batch to batch, although they too are prone to variation due to differences in age and storage.

The equipment hardly differentiates commercial brewers of sahti and homebrewers. Today stainless steel is popular among both. Of the six commercial breweries that focus on sahti, only three are clearly bigger in scale than domestic brewhouses. Commercial brewery Olu Bryki Raum even shares the equipment with homebrewers.

I have tasted outstanding sahti from craft brewers, but in one-time brews the flavor is not always spot-on. Fortunately, Finland has such strict regulation of the Traditional Speciality Guaranteed appellation that inauthentic products are very rare. No equivalent regulations exist in the Baltic States, so what is sold as traditional koduõlu or kaimiškas beer can be anything from highly authentic to a modern beer given a farmhouse twist.

In 2016 I witnessed an intriguing meeting at the craft brewery Panimo Hiisi, in my hometown Jyväskylä. Traditional sahti brewers Maria and Kauko Kuusikko, a daughter-and-father team from Jämijärvi, had been invited to brew an 8.5-barrel (1,000 liters) batch of sahti. The scene that unfolded involved a young, bearded craft brewer arguing with a sixty-year-old sahti master. A few times, I heard the master's words "but that would not be sahti." Kuusikko's long, multistep mash process seemed impossible for the Hiisi brewhouse. After a lengthy discussion, the brewers agreed on a shorter, four-hour mash. Two weeks later, Kuusikko Sahti was served at a local pub, unusually from a real-ale cask. Kauko, who takes the quality of sahti as a very serious matter, was very pleased with the result.

Why Hasn't Sahti Conquered the World Yet?

Often Finnish beer geeks and media complain about the slack commercialization of sahti. If sahti is so unique and special, why hasn't it taken the world by storm? It is hard to accept the answer that the tradition creates excessive difficulties in terms of transportation and shelf life. These were far less of a hurdle a hundred years ago, when sahti was usually consumed in the house where it was brewed.

Just as homemade sahti does, the commercial product requires a cold chain, and the shelf life is measured in weeks. This makes deliveries difficult even in Finland. Finnish pubs sell far more cask-conditioned real ale than sahti. Only two of the most renowned sahti breweries, Lammin Sahti and Finlandia Sahti, deliver regularly to pubs in Finland. Most of the commercial sahti is sold at festivals and at shops and restaurants near the brewery.

Lammin Sahti promises a shelf life of two weeks, knowing that the ale would last much longer if stored as advised. Finlandia Sahti claims a shelf life of eight weeks, assuming that the customers know how to handle the product.

Finnish breweries do get requests from abroad. Lammin Sahti has shipped sahti to several beer festivals elsewhere in Europe and on occasion to the United States. Finlandia Sahti has shipped its ale to Austria and Singapore. For those exporting sahti, the cold transportation is a challenge, and it is important for the receiver to be able to judge whether the ale has arrived in good condition.

Pekka Kääriäinen admits that it would be best for sahti to be brewed locally rather than transported thousands of miles. In any case, sahti should not be sold to drinkers without some background. Receiving a murky and relatively flat beer without a few words about the tradition would leave most customers perplexed.

Remedies to extend shelf life have been suggested. For example, the Finnish craft brewery Pyynikin Käsityöläispanimo makes a hoppy *katajasahti* (9.5 percent ABV) that does not require refrigeration, perhaps thanks to the wort boil with hops. It is brewed in accordance with the rules of the TSG appellation, but the longevity comes at a cost, at least for me: this drink lacks several of the qualities I like in sahti. Another way to address the issue of shelf life would be to use a yeast purified in a lab, but that would be inconsistent with the farmhouse tradition and also the TSG appellation.

WHERE IS SAHTI SOLD IN FINLAND?

The best places for a tourist to sample sahti are beer festivals, medieval fairs, and a few select pubs in larger cities. In Finland, beer above 5.5 percent ABV is sold only in the state-owned liquor store chain Alko or at a brewery shop. Since sahti has at least 6 percent ABV, this considerably limits the options for buying sahti in stores. Only Finlandia Sahti is regularly available in Alko stores, and all the sahti breweries and their shops are outside the cities.

If visiting Finland in summertime, the hardcore beer traveler might consider a visit to the National Sahti Competition. The competition is held in early August, each year at a different location within the traditional sahti districts. Traveling there requires some effort, but the reward is being able to sample forty to fifty homemade sahtis and meet the brewers.

Lammin Sahti

Pekka Kääriäinen's parents did not brew sahti, but a helping hand is always close by in the sahti districts. Under a neighbor's tutelage, Kääriäinen made his first sahti at the age of fourteen. The bug stayed with him. At Helsinki School of Economics, he wrote his master's thesis on commercial production of sahti wort. At the time, Lammin Sahti, which he had founded with wife Sirpa in 1985, was about to start selling wort, as a work-around because the authorities had thus far been reluctant to grant alcohol production licenses.

One day Pekka Kääriäinen saw a television news item about another brewing company, now-defunct Joutsan Sahti, which was proudly showing off its license application. He obtained a video recording of the news and paused it when the screen showed the application form. Working from this frame of video, he prepared a similar application. Somewhat unexpectedly, the two companies were granted licenses on the same date in 1987. Lammin Sahti sold the first commercial sahti, beating rival Joutsan Sahti by one month.

The spent grains from sahti retain plenty of sugars, and Lammin Sahti has an ingenious way of utilizing them. The brewery makes a lower-strength sahti-like ale from the later runnings and then distills that ale. The spirit is aged in oak casks and would qualify as whisky, but Kääriäinen prefers to call it "Spirit of Sahti," implying that it is distilled sahti. This fine 40-percent spirit drinks like a malt whisky with an herbal scent of forest.

Today Lammin Sahti produces 250 barrels (30,000 liters) of sahti a year, which makes it the biggest commercial producer. Nevertheless, the sahti operation is now a sideline business for a company that manages several bars and cafes, as well as the Suuret Oluet—Pienet Panimot (Great Beers—Small Breweries) beer festival, held each summer in several Finnish cities. The largest volumes of the sahti are sold at summer festivals, along with the brewery shop and the company's other establish-ments. A small share goes to pubs and restaurants.

The stainless steel brewhouse is similar in design to a domestic farm-house brewery but scaled to 11-barrel (1,300-liter) batch size. The brew-ery even has "the world's biggest kuurna," holding 17 barrels (2,000 liters) of mash. The wort is not boiled, and the maximum temperature for the mash and wort is 176°F (80°C). Lammin Sahti's fermentation with fresh Finnish baker's yeast is quite typical: one to two days at room tempera-ture followed by maturation at lower temperatures. The ale is ready two weeks from brewing.

The brewery's flagship product, the eponymous Lammin Sahti, is made to a gravity of 20°P, with an alcohol content of 7.5 percent. Pekka Kääriäinen considers juniper an essential part of sahti, and he takes great care in selecting the branches. Hops are not used. The malt bill features 5 percent dark rye malt and 95 percent Sahti Malt. The propor-tion of dark rye is perhaps less than average for the region of Lammi, but he finds that using dark malt with restraint brings out the maltiness better.

Lammin Sahti is a classic example of a sahti with well-defined layers of flavors. An obvious banana aroma hits the nose first, and the first sip delivers a firm fresh, bready, and toffeeish maltiness, finishing with del-icate yet noticeable herbal juniper. This reddish-brown ale is fairly hazy two weeks after brewing, but at four weeks it can be almost bright.

Finlandia Sahti

Antti Vesala built Finlandia Sahti in 1992 in an old cowshed in Forssa. He was an engineer and apparently fond of Rube Goldberg–style machines. He designed and crafted the equipment himself, including an ingenious machine built from a huge laundry spin-dryer that centrifuges the wort out from the malt.

Petteri Lähdeniemi and Auli Mattila bought Finlandia Sahti in 2011, when Vesala retired. Lähdeniemi began as a homebrewer who, as a farm-er's son, had access to old unused farmstead buildings. The brewery was rebuilt in a more western location in Sastamala, again in an old cowshed. Lähdeniemi had never brewed sahti before, but he assiduously adapted all of Vesala's equipment, methods, and recipes, and people old enough to

Finlandia Sahti's brewery and the brewpub are so deep in the countryside that on my way there I thought I was lost a few miles before the destination. Yet the brewpub attracts both Finnish and international groups.

remember generally agree that the taste hasn't changed much since 1995, when Vesala sold his own sahti for the first time.

Vesala learned to brew in Orimattila, in the eastern reaches of sahti country, which probably accounts for the fact that Finlandia Sahti is made solely from barley malt. Its reddish-brown color comes from caramel malt. The brew receives additions of juniper infusion and a small quantity of homegrown hops. As is usual for sahti, the fermentation relies on the standard Finnish baker's yeast.

On brew day, the mash is boiled, but the wort remains unboiled. The wort is first cooled to 50°F (10°C) but then slowly heated until the yeast ramps up its action and ferments at ambient brewhouse temperature. Accordingly, fermentation temperature and time both vary with the season. After primary fermentation, the sahti undergoes intensive cold conditioning for at least two weeks.

Finlandia Sahti at 8 percent ABV is dark reddish brown in color and not effervescent. The nose is filled with an obvious banana aroma, Christmas spices, and alcohol warmth. Then come the malty flavors of toffee, caramel, and bread. Perhaps because of boiling the mash and conditioning in the cold, the body is lighter than average, though still robust. In addition to this, the brewery makes a stronger, 10-percent version of Finlandia Sahti, which is brewed in the same way except for the higher gravity and alcohol content.

Lähdeniemi delivers the sahti himself, and his distribution routes can be as long as 430 miles (700 kilometers). Over forty Alko stores compose the main market. Selected pubs, the brewpub, and the summer festival circuit make up a smaller share. Because of the diligence in deliveries, Finlandia provides the first sahti experience for many. The Finlandia facility's yearly output of sahti is around 170 barrels (20,000 liters), and the brewery makes a small amount of modern-style craft beer too.

Nearby cheese producer Herkkujuustola makes a delicious washed-rind cheese, Sahti Vilho, washed with Finlandia Sahti.

Hollolan Hirvi

Hollolan Hirvi is famous for its Kivisahti (literally "stone sahti"), brewed with an ancient method of adding hot stones to the mash. It is brewed in 40-gallon (150-liter) batches, and only around ten batches are made each year. Hence, this classic is a rare sight even in Finland.

The brewery is nestled in the countryside of Hollola, where it was built in an old cowshed in 1999. Most of the ale is sold in an adjoining restaurant, which specializes in moose dishes along with sahti. The restaurant is open primarily on demand for groups and for celebrations such as weddings. In summertime it is open to all on one day a week. Most Kivisahti is sold in the restaurant and for selected Finnish beer festivals. In 2015 a fabulous smoke sauna (see chapter 8, page 112) for visitors to bathe in was added to the venue.

The founder, Ilkka Sipilä, talks proudly of the long-standing traditions of his family on this land. According to oral tradition, sahti has been brewed where his house stands for more than five hundred years. Brewing with stones is both local and family tradition. Sipilä reported that his grandmother, the family's sahti master, was taken once a year to a stone pit to choose new brewing stones.

Sipilä brews with stones intended for sauna stoves that do not shatter so easily. He heats the stones in a wood fire until they glow with heat, and he drops them into the mash at the end of mashing. I have seen this once and it is an impressive sight, with plumes of mash splashing high into the air. In the old days, the stones provided plenty of heat for the mash, but the number of stones for Kivisahti is fairly small, and they contribute little to heating. What the stones do bring is a delicate flavor of smoke and burnt caramel.

Kivisahti is brewed to a gravity of 20°P and alcohol content of 6.5 percent from barley malt, dark rye malt, juniper infusion, hops from Sipilä's yard, and Finnish baker's yeast. Both the mash and the lautering steps are carried out in an electrically heated kettle similar to many homebrewers'. The mash is brought to a boil, but the wort is not boiled.

Ilkka Sipilä says that he grew up in the sahti tradition, and he claims to have tasted sahti at four years of age, long before his first lemonade. Sipilä uses these tongs for lifting glowing hot stones into the mash.

Primary fermentation in warm conditions takes one to two days, and then the ale matures in the cold for three to four weeks.

Sipilä does not strive for consistency, and Kivisahti is delightfully different each time, as many domestic sahtis are. Sometimes it tastes fairly sweet, while sometimes it has pleasant rustic tartness that should not be mistaken for the sour taint of an old sahti. Some people have had difficulties in recognizing the flavor imparted by the stones, but having tasted this ale several times and at different ages, I can attest that there is always a hint of smoke and burnt mash in the flavor.

Olu Bryki Raum

For decades Jouko Ylijoki has interviewed farmhouse folks about traditional ales, and he has a million stories to tell. His brewery, Olu Bryki Raum, bakes those stories into liquid bread. Each year, the brewery produces around 30 barrels (3,500 liters) of traditional ales, which are sold mainly at beer festivals and medieval fairs. This brewery is more about promoting culture than about business.

Ylijoki is very enthusiastic about medieval fairs, and I have never seen him without a Viking Age costume on. Each summer, he demonstrates the ancient brewing methods at a few fairs, where spectators can buy his old-time ales too.

The brewery has two locations in Isojoki, and usually the brewer at both of them is a renowned local sahti master, Esa Kivioja. A brewhouse with a capacity of 3.4 barrels (400 liters) is in an old dairy. This space is dedicated to the flagship ale, Kullervo Ruissahti. The other ales are brewed at the facility of the Sahtiopisto (Sahti Academy) with the same equipment used by domestic sahti brewers. A portion of the malt bill for Olu Bryki Raum's ales is filled by malting at the Sahtiopisto brewery.

This brewery makes several traditional ales, but perhaps the most distinctive member of the family is Kullervo Ruissahti. The name denotes a rye sahti, traditionally made with a large proportion of unmalted rye in the areas around Isojoki. The recipe comes from the family of Esa Kivioja. Kullervo has a gravity of 25 to 26°P and an alcohol content around 7.5 percent. The malt bill is a 50:50 blend of unmalted rye and pale barley malt.

Jouko Ylijoki at the Turku Medieval Market in 2016. This annual medieval fair attracts more than 150,000 visitors each year. COURTESY OF SAMI BRODKIN

Because of the high proportion of unmalted grains, Ylijoki mashes for sixteen to eighteen hours with ascending temperature. The mash ends in a boil that lasts at least half an hour. The wort is not boiled. In the kuurna, Ylijoki likes to use straw along with juniper branches, because he considers straw to add to the flavor. The ale has a clear taste of juniper, and Ylijoki believes that it results from slow lautering, when the mash is resting for hours on a bed of juniper. Ruissahti is fermented with Finnish baker's yeast at 68°F (20°C) for two to three days, and it then matures in the cold.

This ale can be sold at two weeks, but Ylijoki prefers it at one month. The nose brings a grain harvest to mind with its subtle notes of straw alongside banana. Slight sweetness in the taste accompanies a grainy flavor of rye porridge and lingering juniper. The mouthfeel is incredibly viscous and oily, which surprises the drinker every time.

Sahtikrouvi

At Sahtikrouvi, in Hartola, ballroom dances such as the waltz and tango are lubricated with sahti. And you can sleep there too, because this place is a combination of dance hall, sahti brewpub, and campsite. The sahti is sold mainly at the brewpub and at a few local summer festivals.

The 10-barrel (1,200-liter) brewery designed by founder and brewer Matti Punakallio is no less exotic than the business concept. Both mashing and lautering take place in a cylindrical vessel that seems to be sitting on its side, reminiscent of a concrete mixer. Other inventions here include a 210-gallon (800-liter) serving tank on wheels for selling sahti at bigger festivals. This place has quite a pedigree—the brewpub opened in 1996, but Punakallio has sold sahti wort since 1983.

Sahtikrouvi makes a sturdy sahti with a gravity of 23.5°P and 9 percent ABV. It is brewed in the style of the eastern sahti districts solely

Matti Punakallio and his combined mash and lauter tun. The outer drum revolves much in the manner of a concrete mixer.

Sahtikrouvi attracts hundreds of dancers every Friday in summertime. Finnish men are sometimes said to be reluctant to dance, but after a hefty glassful of sahti, they are ready to tango.

from barley with dark caramel malt for reddish-brown color. The brew contains neither hops nor juniper. The wort is boiled for half an hour, which produces a slightly more beer-like sahti, reminiscent of some dark, strong Belgian beers. The taste is very malty, with a warming alcohol, flavors of dark dried fruits, and wine-gum-like fruitiness. It is dangerously drinkable, especially as it slips down glass after glass while one is dancing.

Sahti Around the World

Craft brewers often share a passion to explore the wealth of world beer styles, and sahti is certainly one of the most unusual and distinct styles to delve into. As of 2018, the beer rating site RateBeer.com lists more than forty commercial non-Finnish beers that are either inspired by sahti or attempts to re-create authentic sahti. Many of these are onetime brews and only locally available.

As explained in the chapter "Drinking Sahti," sahti is not a geographically bounded designation. Finnish ingredients aren't absolutely neces-

Arvet Väli showing visitors around at the Pihtla Õlleköök brewery in Saaremaa, Estonia. The brewery's traditional koduõlu, Taako Pihtla Õlu, would pass as a sahti as well.

sary for authenticity either. With commitment and solid understanding of the tradition, a genuine sahti can be brewed anywhere.

That said, in some brews marketed as sahti, rye and juniper on the ingredient list are the only connection to the concept of sahti. These brews may be standard modern ales made with "a few changes to the traditional sahti recipe" and "more appealing for a modern audience." That is regrettable, because it renders the tradition less clear and misleads customers.

Nevertheless, authentic sahti and exciting sahti-inspired ales are being brewed outside Finland. For instance, after a friend of mine sampled a locally made sahti at the Goose Island brewpub in Chicago, he reported that it tasted authentic. Also, the Polish-made sahti Pinta Koniec Świata tasted genuine to me.

In 2018 RateBeer's highest rated beer in the category Sahti/Gotlandsdricke/Koduõlu was the Ale Apothecary's Sahati. While this seems to be a misclassification, the ale still can be rightly called sahti-inspired, even though definitely not a traditional sahti, gotlandsdricke, or koduõlu. Of course, it is worth bearing in mind that the beer classification on rating sites is normally done by the users, not the brewery. Just as brewers themselves do, drinkers vary greatly in perspective, particularly with regard to the more special or exotic styles.

Tucked away in a mountainous and forested part of Bend, Oregon, the Ale Apothecary could easily be mistaken for a farmhouse brewery. Indeed, many visitors have drawn this conclusion, although founder Paul Arney has clarified that the actual farms are far away. Branches from Engelmann spruces on the brewery's property are used in Sahati, in much the same way juniper branches are in sahti. Arney has even hollowed out a 1.5-barrel kuurna from a spruce trunk with his own hands, and earlier versions of Sahati were lautered through the spruce boughs in this kuurna. When the brewery graduated to a three-barrel system, Arney discovered that the same resiny and citrussy flavor can be achieved by adding spruce branches to the mash. While the wooden kuurna is no longer used, it is still displayed with pride at the brewery's tasting room.

Sahati is an 11 percent ABV ale brewed with Vienna malt, rye, aged hops, and spruce branches. The wort for it is boiled for two to three hours, but the brewery also produces a sour ale without a wort boil, called Vamonos. Sahati is fermented with airborne yeast and microbes, then aged for two years. This puts its fermentation more in line with the Belgian farmhouse ale tradition. I haven't been able to taste it yet, but this sure sounds like a beer worth hunting for.

Such intrepid brewers need not venture into the world of sahti on their own. Several Finnish sahti ambassadors have done their part in spreading the specialist brewing know-how. Pekka Kääriäinen has brewed sahti with OEC Brewing in Connecticut, and with New Belgium and BJ's Restaurant & Brewhouse, both in Colorado. Also, Markku Pulliainen from Finland's Malmgård Brewery created a collaboratively brewed sahti with Dock Street Brewery in Philadelphia.

Brewing sahti on a different continent has brought a few surprises for the Finnish sahti masters. Kääriäinen tried juniper branches from several locations in the USA but found the flavor from all of them piney and woody, lacking the herbal qualities of Finnish juniper. Ever since, he has carried dried chips of Finnish juniper in his suitcase when involved in overseas brews. Other ingredients too can present obstacles. Pulliainen mailed fresh Finnish baker's yeast to Philadelphia, only to find out that the delivery took sixteen days instead of the promised six. When the yeast finally arrived, it wasn't fresh at all and made a poor sahti. Pulliainen's first encounter with American juniper didn't go without surprises either, as the story on page 135 demonstrates.

Finally, commercial ales similar to sahti can be found in Estonia and Lithuania, though the farmhouse breweries that create them are not mimicking the Finnish approach. For example, traditional Estonian breweries Pihtla Õlleköök and Pihtla Pruulikoda make rustic koduõlus that would comply with the TSG appellation of sahti.

- 7 -

Low-Alcohol Farmhouse Ales

Nourishment for Work

FARMHOUSE FOLK OF THE PAST could not afford to turn their grains into the best ale very often, and sahti was reserved for feasts and visits from prestigious guests. There were various other kinds of ales for day-to-day life. These were typically low enough in alcohol that the whole family could drink them as part of the regular diet and nourishment for work.

In the sahti districts of western Finland, everyday ales were often more dilute and frugal versions of the feast ales. The techniques were the same as for sahti overall, but these ordinary "small beers" were made with lower effort, less malt, and a higher proportion of unmalted grains. Whenever strong ale was brewed, the residual sugars were rinsed from the spent mash and turned into a low-alcohol ale. However, this was not the main approach for creating everyday ales, because the strong feast ales were typically brewed only a few times a year.

In the eastern stretches of Finland, sahti was an alien drink, and the people on farms there made their own style of ales for both feasts and daily use. The eastern ales fit well into the categories *gruel beers, porridge beers, bread-mash beers,* and *oven beers*—these kinds of beverages are so obscure that established terminology does not exist. That is a pity because they seem to give a glimpse into what the first beers of humankind were like. Although sahti is known as a primitive ale, it soon becomes clear that sahti is far from the most primitive beer there is.

Porridge or beer? This can be enjoyed as both. It is a special "beer porridge" that makes an ancient ale when diluted with water and fermented. Perhaps this is how brewing got started at the dawn of civilization. MIKA LAITINEN

The beverages I'm about to discuss are not even always considered beers. To straighten things out, I'll start with my definition: beer is a cereal-based fermented alcoholic beverage with at least some of the fermentable sugars coming from the cereals. This is an articulate definition, but it does not prevent things from getting really fuzzy. Some of the most archaic ales have existed in both alcoholic and nonalcoholic versions. Ancient fermentation was often mixed with yeast and souring bacteria, and the proportions of these microbes cast the ale into sour nonalcoholic beverages and intoxicating drinks. The fact remains, we cannot always tell whether our ancestors brewed beer with a buzz or just a nourishing cereal beverage. This is one of the key issues in the early history of beer.

Late-Runnings Ales

After collecting the richest, first wort for the feast ale, the brewer may keep on rinsing the mash with hot water or juniper infusion, to obtain more diluted late runnings of wort. These runnings capture the residual malt sugars and can be fermented into a lower-alcohol ale.

The brewer has plenty of leeway in how dilute the resulting ale will be. In the past, the late runnings were collected in volumes up to one and a half times that of the sahti, which would make a very weak ale. Today those who even bother to collect late runnings will stop at considerably less.

At first the late runnings can still be of considerable gravity, and they can be collected for what is known as *ladies' sahti*, which is a sweet and malty but only slightly fermented ale. When women were expected to drink less alcohol, this kind of ale was served at feasts alongside sahti. The practice remained alive as recently as the 1960s. Sometimes ladies' sahti was made from the first runnings as standard sahti was, but taking the best portion of the late runnings was perhaps more typical. Now ladies too express a preference for "proper sahti," so this tradition is seldom seen today.

Late-runnings ale is usually fermented very briefly, just to preserve the brew and produce a slight fizz. The ale is typically cellared within a few hours after visible fermentation begins, and it will be ready to drink within a day or two.

Another almost effortless way to utilize the spent mash is an ale known as *taari* in Finland, or *taar* in Estonia. I thought that this tradi-

Kalju Sinijärv, from Saaremaa, and his taar. The spent mash is fermented in a lautering vat, and the next day taar can be drawn from the tap (by lifting the wooden pole).

tion died before the Second World War, until I was unexpectedly served a cup of taar while touring the farmhouse breweries of Saaremaa in 2015.

I was visiting local brewmaster Kalju Sinijärv and enjoying his excellent koduõlu. While I was busily writing my notes, he went to a shed and came back with a scoop of a hazy yellow drink, which had an aroma of straw and barnyard. The ale tasted dry and tart, with notes of lemon, yogurt, and butter. Sinijärv said that this drink, taar, doesn't contain any alcohol, and it did taste more like a lactic fermentation. Perhaps there was a little alcohol, but below the taste threshold. Clearly this was not a fancy celebration ale, more like good refreshment amid one's daily chores.

Sinijärv explained the brewing process, and it matched Finnish descriptions of the early twentieth century perfectly. After the first wort has been taken for koduõlu or sahti, the tap of the lautering vat is closed and hot water is poured onto the spent grains. Then the lautering vat is left as it is, and fermentation soon starts spontaneously. Taar is ready the next day, and can be drawn simply by opening the tap. The ale remains in the lautering vat until it is all consumed, or becomes undrinkable.

Confusingly, the name "taari" or "taar" spans a whole bunch of farm-house ales. It has been made in several alternative ways—for instance, by fermenting a pristine mash (not the spent grains) or with the malt bread technique described in the next section. Some versions have even been strong in alcohol. It seems that fermenting the mash first and sieving out the grain solids just before drinking is the common denominator.

The Oven Beers of Eastern Finland

Today many Finnish cafeterias and households serve the low-alcohol malt beverage kalja with food. Usually it is made in the kitchen, though versions are sold commercially. This sweet beverage with tastes of rye bread is generally regarded as a soft drink, and even many children drink it. Few realize that today's kalja is a modernized version of an ancient farmhouse ale, once especially familiar in eastern Finland.

Modern kalja is made from dark rye malt, sugar, and baker's yeast. The main ingredient, dark rye malt known as Tuoppi Kaljamallas, is read-ily available at Finnish supermarkets. Actually, this same malt appears in

Ordinary lunch at a Finnish workplace cafeteria often includes a glass of kalja.
MIKA LAITINEN

most sahtis for darker color and background notes of rye bread. Today's kalja is very simple to brew with ordinary cooking skills and kitchenware: mix the rye malt and sugar into hot water, allow to cool, add baker's yeast, ferment very briefly, and move into a cool location while the ale is still sweet and largely unfermented. The alcohol content is usually not more than 1 percent ABV.

In today's kalja, sugar is a shortcut to sweetness, which in the old days came from malted and unmalted grains. Converting grain starches into sugars is a laborious task, and traditional ways of brewing kalja went into decline as soon as cheap sugar became widely available. Also similar traditional farmhouse beverages—such as kali in Estonia, kvass further east in Europe, and gira in Lithuania—are now mostly sugar-powered beverages.

Many Finnish farmhouses were still making kalja without sugar in the early twentieth century. As far as I know, these farmhouse traditions are now extinct in Finland, so I will review them on the basis of Finnish ethnographic accounts and my own brewing experiments. It should be borne in mind, though, that the old brewing practices were hugely varied, and what I refer to as kalja was known by several other names as well, such as *vaassa*. The taari referred to above is another part of this picture.

Usually, traditional kalja contained both raw and malted grains, but their ratio varied vastly. A festive version might have been all malt, and there was a very frugal variant called *jauhokalja* (literally "flour beer"), which was made from nothing but unmalted flour, water, and yeast. Two parts of unmalted rye and one part of rye malt would have been a fairly typical base for eastern Finnish kalja. Rye was by far the most popular grain and often the only grain used. Oats were fairly common too, and perhaps even more popular than barley.

Some brewers used juniper branches as a filtering aid, and occasionally a handful of hops was thrown into the brew, but often the ingredient list consisted of just malted and unmalted grains, water, and perhaps yeast. Sometimes leftover potatoes or pieces of bread were added to the brew.

The heart of a traditional eastern Finnish house is a massive oven, which in the past was used to prepare the bulk of the food: plenty of breads, porridges, stews, and pies. Kalja was just another food that was brewed—or should I say baked—in the oven. Usually kalja was made once a week, taking the form of bread along the way.

My first attempt to make traditional Finnish kalja. This rye porridge was baked in the oven, diluted with water, and fermented with baker's yeast. The ale tasted very gruel-like—not particularly delicious but certainly nourishing. MIKA LAITINEN

This is the main distinction between the farmhouse brewing traditions of western and eastern Finland. While the westerners have brewed with dedicated brewing equipment in the outbuildings, the easterners have brewed in their kitchen or similar facilities, mostly with standard cookware. In the east, a wooden cask or bucket for keeping the ale was about the only vessel dedicated solely to brewing.

Brewing kalja began by mixing grains and water in a metal cauldron or clay pot. Then the porridge-like mixture was kept warm for several hours, usually in the oven, and sometimes by the stove. In essence, this was a mashing step, but it was never referred to that way. Instead, the eastern Finns called it *sweetening*, and it continued until the porridge became darker and indeed tasted sweet. The sweetening usually took at least six hours, because of the high proportion of unmalted grains and the uncontrolled temperatures.

Usually the sweetening was given its finishing touches by baking the porridge in the oven. The baking was done in either a cauldron or a clay pot much like a casserole dish, or the dough was formed into large loaves

Another of my experiments with creating traditional Finnish kalja. This time, I baked unmalted and malted rye into sweet loaves of dark bread. A successful test brew with them was done at the Medieval Market of Turku in 2018. COURTESY OF SAMI BRODKIN

of bread that were then baked. Whether involving porridge or bread, the baking was complete when the crust had turned brown, which would give a pleasing brown color to the ale.

The sweetening was done in a highly concentrated form, and the grains were later diluted with water. The simplest method was to just pour the porridge or crumble the malt bread into a wooden cask and mix it with water. Often the ale was fermented with grain solids without a lautering step. The heavier solids fell to the bottom, and casks intended for kalja drew out the ale from a tap above the dregs.

With this method, a large amount of sediment was left at the bottom of the cask. As the level of kalja dropped, the cask was topped up with water, for getting more out of the sediment. The resulting weaker ale was drunk, and the cycle of topping up and drinking was repeated several times, until the beverage was unpalatable. The disgust with several-cycle-old kalja has been immortalized in many sayings, such as "like the seventh water over the top of kalja" for describing something absolutely worthless.

Usually kalja was fermented with yeast harvested from the previous batch or with a sourdough starter used for baking, and later commercial baker's yeast entered use. Meanwhile, some brewers allowed the brew to ferment spontaneously. Fermentation times were typically very short, and the kalja was ready to drink within a day or two.

Since eastern Finns didn't have sahti, they used the kalja technique also for celebration drinks, though in a more refined manner. The amount of grains was bumped up, as was the proportion of malt. A lautering stage was sometimes added to filter out the grain solids before fermentation. While everyday kalja was never made with alcohol in mind, the feast version was sometimes slightly heady.

Kalja was made also in a few parts of western Finland, because the process was easily adapted to the weekly routines of the household. However, it was regarded as a second-rate ale by westerners, as manifested in sayings like "kalja is for working, and sahti is for feasting." As usual, ethnographic accounts say very little about the actual taste of the old-style farmhouse kalja. Typical descriptors are "tart," "sour," and "sweet and sour." Clearly, souring bacteria played a role.

The Broader Landscape of Oven Beers

The kalja style of folk ales has been made across vast expanses of Europe and beyond, and it spans a great many cultures. I would now like to lay out a vague theory as to how these ales are linked to the beers of ancient civilizations. We are getting into a gray area here, since the histories of these kinds of indigenous ales are poorly documented, and theories of how ancient Sumerians and Egyptians brewed therefore remain unproven. Nevertheless, this topic is far too juicy to be ignored. I'm not certainly the first to suggest that oven-baked folk beers are linked to the prehistory of beer, but perhaps I can provide a sharper explanation why there seems to be a kinship.

These folk ales are brewed from various cereals, depending on what is locally available. Nonetheless, these features define an obvious kinship:

- The ale is often made from both raw and malted grains, typically with a large proportion of unmalted cereals. Additional flavorings play a minor role or are not used at all.

- Brewing does not follow today's conventional malting–mashing–lautering procedure. Instead, it often begins with making porridge or bread, which is later mixed with water. The process can be completed without large vessels for mashing, lautering, or boiling. In fact, the process is likely a remnant from times when crafting large vessels was difficult.
- Lautering is optional, and the ale is often fermented with the grain solids. The solids may be sieved out right after fermentation, or somehow avoided just before drinking. A lautering step for separating wort from grain solids may be used for more important occasions. If the process includes a wort-making step, the wort is left unboiled.
- The ale can be made in both alcoholic and nonalcoholic forms. Fermentation may be initiated with a sourdough starter or dregs from a previous batch, and more recent practices have incorporated baker's yeast. Mixed fermentation with yeast and lactic bacteria is typical.
- Often fermentation is merely a preservation method. The process may not be fine-tuned for converting all grain starch into sugars, and the final beer may contain starch. When these drinks are made merely for nourishment, lactic bacteria dominates the fermentation.
- Many of these folk ales have been modernized fairly recently through the use of sugar instead of the traditional process involving grains.

These are typical features of traditional kalja, and the old traditions of Estonian kali seem to be identical to those for Finnish kalja. In Estonia's Setomaa region, this style of ale is still brewed from a specially baked malt bread, though the brewers use sugar too. Brewing from a malt bread is still a living tradition in Lithuania as well, where this style of ale is called *keptinis*. Today the malt-bread ales of Setomaa and Lithuania usually contain more than a few percent of alcohol.

Eastern European kvass partly overlaps this category. The traditional versions made from ordinary bread are more like lactic fermented foodstuffs, and making these drinks can be hardly called brewing. Another way of making kvass, involving unmalted flour and a portion of malt, bears closer resemblance to kalja. It seems that in Russia the word kvass has been reserved for nonalcoholic cereal beverages, while there are other alive Russian oven beers that do contain alcohol.

Another traditional folk ale of this kind is boza or bouza, which is still brewed in both nonalcoholic and alcoholic versions in parts of the Middle East, Central Asia, North Africa, and the Balkans. Most of today's recipes from the Balkans, Turkey, and Egypt include sugar, but it seems that the traditional techniques starting with unmalted and malted cereals have not been forgotten. Depending on the area, boza is made from a whole host of grains—such as millet, wheat, barley, maize, and sorghum—but this broad spectrum can't obscure the fact that the brewing process of some variants bears a close resemblance to that used for kalja.

In the early fourth century AD, the Greek alchemist Zosimus wrote down an Egyptian beer recipe, which is virtually identical to some versions of present-day boza: Barley is germinated and then ground and baked into loaves, which are later crumbled into water. The recipe gives two options: grain solids are sieved out either before or after fermentation.

The history of boza might extend much further into the past of ancient Egypt and Mesopotamia, but that path comes with much speculation, as do the theories of how ancient Sumerians, Babylonians, and Egyptians brewed. Although those theories have found their way into many beer books, scientists don't seem to agree on how these folk of the distant past brewed their beer. Nonetheless, it is commonly thought that both in Sumer and in ancient Egypt the brewing often involved malt and some other cereal product. Whether this other ingredient was just unmalted grains or some kind of beer bread is subject to debate.

Another thing muddying the waters is that surely the ancient Sumerians and Egyptians brewed in myriad ways. If the brewing techniques were highly varied across the sparsely populated countryside of Finland in around 1900, how great the multitude of traditions there must have been in ancient Mesopotamia and Egypt over three thousand years!

If we map the areas where these folk ales have been brewed, we get a contiguous area that starts in North Africa and extends through Turkey, the Balkans, and Eastern Europe into the Baltic States and eastern Finland. Further east, the areas include the Middle East and parts of Central and Northern Asia. It certainly seems that this family of ales started spreading early on from the Middle East, where farming began.

Despite the similarities, it is also entirely possible that the northern oven beers were discovered independently of the cultures of the Middle East. In fact, archaeological and historical evidence suggest that the big ovens where these beers have been traditionally made became popular in the north only in the second millennium.

~ II ~

THE CRAFT OF A FARMHOUSE BREWER

A domestic sahti brewery on a farmstead in Sysmä.

— 8 —

Grain and Malt

Once Brewers Did It All Themselves

I N THE EARLY TWENTIETH CENTURY, most sahti brewers were still self-sufficient in their ingredients. They brewed from grains that grew well on their land and made for good ale. For a farmhouse brewer, making good malt was as important a skill as brewing good beer. Therefore, to understand farmhouse ale, or beers of the past for that matter, we need to understand how farmhouse brewers have selected and malted their grains.

Today most Nordic and Baltic farmhouse ales are made with commercial malt, which marks a considerable change in the tradition and a sad loss. We are fortunate that the bulk of the knowledge has survived, offering a clear view of ancient ways of preparing grains.

Grain Varieties

In Finland barley and rye have been the most important crops for a millennium, and these are the major brewing grains for sahti too. While in some districts sahti is made solely from barley malt, most sahtis contain both barley and rye.

Barley has been the favorite brewing grain through the ages, and it was among the first crops when farming began in Europe. The cultivation of rye gained popularity in the Nordic region during the Viking Age (AD 800–1050); it has been a staple food since. In 2016 Finns voted for their national food, and the winner was rye bread.

Steeping barley at Viking Malt in Lahti. The principles of malting have remained the same for thousands of years.

While barley malt generally yields sweet and mellow beer, rye imparts a drier, grainier, and more assertive flavor. Rye also contains lots of gummy compounds called beta glucans, which make the beer viscous and full-bodied. Beers with larger amounts of rye, 20 percent or more of the grain, are often an acquired taste.

Most present-day sahti brewers add 5 to 10 percent rye to the grain bill. However, usually this addition is done with the particular dark rye malt called Kaljamallas, which even in small proportions gives a reddish-brown color and a pronounced taste of dark rye bread.

Ethnographic surveys of the past reveal that the percentage of rye used to be higher, when farmers still brewed from their own grains. Before the 1960s, using a quarter rye wasn't exceptional, and half-and-half recipes of barley and rye weren't rare either. In some areas, rye even challenged barley as the main brewing grain.

It seems that sahti folks have usually liked the flavor combination of barley and rye, but agricultural matters have surely played a role in the grain choices too. Rye is a hardy grain that thrives in poor soils, and for some fields it is a better choice. On the other hand, some cultivars of barley are even more cold-hardy than rye. Farming both of these grains added diversity that ensured a satisfactory harvest. As I explained in the chapter "Drinking Sahti," the proportions of barley and rye vary regionally, and I suspect that these preferences stem mostly from agricultural conditions.

Wheat and oats too have been used in northern farmhouse ales, but mostly as a substitute for barley or as a small supplement. In coastal Norway, where barley does not always grow well, ales were sometimes brewed even entirely from oat malt. Today some sahti brewers fine-tune their recipes with 5 to 10 percent oats or wheat, usually in unmalted form.

In general, northern farmhouse brewers have favored all-malt ales, but Finns for some reason have been more inclined to supplement the malt bill with a share of unmalted grains. Fairly often, traditional sahti recipes feature small amounts of unmalted grains as well, usually rye. Elsewhere in the Nordic and Baltic countries, the use of unmalted grains seems to be very rare. In Saaremaa, Estonia, I asked a koduõlu brewer whether the locals brew with unmalted cereals. He raised his eyebrows and replied emphatically, "Beer is made from malt."

Brewers around Isojoki formerly used an extremely large proportion of unmalted rye, and as recently as the 1980s the majority of the grain

Malts typically used in sahti: pale barley malt (top), pale rye malt (left), and a dark rye malt known as Kaljamallas (bottom).

bill consisted of unmalted rye. Jouko Ylijoki, an expert in Nordic folk ales, nicknamed this unusual brew *grain sahti*. Today most brewers in Isojoki prefer malted rye, but occasionally they brew these extreme ales for presentation's sake. Once in Isojoki, I tasted a sahti made from 70 percent unmalted rye. It had a very grainy taste and an extremely viscous mouthfeel—definitely an acquired taste.

Grain sahti demands highly unusual brewing techniques. Modern brewing books tell us that unmalted cereals are adjuncts that can be used for up to 50 percent of the grain bill. What these books don't say is that if you use extremely long mashing times, from twelve to eighteen hours, the starches will be converted to sugars even with 90 percent unmalted rye and 10 percent barley malt. Apparently the farmhouse brewers found this out by trial and error.

Farmhouse Malting

The basic principles of malting have remained the same for thousands of years, with the process consisting of steeping, germination, and drying phases. However, in every phase the routines and preferences of the malt-ster have a notable effect on the malt character, which, in turn, affects the taste of the ale. Surveys of the past reveal enormous variety in the farm-house malting practices, which surely have induced diverse house flavors.

In the years after World War II, farmhouse malting was still fairly common in Finland, but by the end of the 1960s virtually all sahti brew-ers were using commercial malt. The old malting practices were recorded in heritage surveys, but, because techniques were so varied and not all details were captured, it is a bit tricky to figure out what the malt was like and what kind of ale it yielded. Fortunately, parallel traditions have been documented and even preserved in Norway. In the 2000s, some sahti

A Finnish smoke sauna from the early twentieth century. In the past, this kind of bathhouse was used for malting as well. The malt was spread on the bathing platform, and the wood-heated stove on the right provided a drying heat. In case you are wondering, the men bathing here are holding birch whisks, which are used to increase the effect of the steam and whip the dirt off. UNKNOWN PHOTOGRAPHER, COURTESY OF HELSINKI CITY MUSEUM

brewers have revived home malting, but to my knowledge nobody malts in the most traditional way, in a *smoke sauna* or drying barn.

In farmhouses, steeping typically lasted one to three days. Sacks of grain were often steeped in a river, spring, or lake. Sometimes grains were also soaked indoors in wooden vats. Then the grains were germinated, either still in the sacks, on floors or other wooden surfaces, or in shallow wooden vessels. Germination took at least two days, and drying started when the shoots had grown to an appropriate length. Usually the shoot had to reach the length of the kernel, but many other rules for ending the germination have been used as well.

In Finland malt was usually dried either in a drying barn called a *riihi* or in a smoke sauna. The riihi was devoted to threshing and drying grains, while the smoke sauna was a multifunctional building used for bathing, malting, brewing, curing meat, and giving birth, among other things. The principles of drying were similar between these buildings: Heat was generated by a massive wood-heated stove without a chimney. The hot smoke filled the room, and it was occasionally vented through a small hatch. Moist grains were spread out on the shelves in the upper parts of the room.

Drying usually took two or three days, during which time the grains needed to be monitored and turned regularly. Night and day, someone had to keep the heat up and watch for overheating. In Finland this task was often given to the youth, and sometimes youngsters from nearby turned up there to provide company at nighttime. Malt saunas were known to be places of storytelling, singing, and romances—the nightclubs of the time.

Finnish farmhouse maltsters had two distinct approaches to drying malt. In the first method, wet germinated grains were spread thinly in the riihi or sauna, with the maltster applying gentle heat at first and then raising the heat toward the end of the drying. Similar ascending heating is used today for producing pale malt, and it is known to preserve the enzymes well.

In the second method, grains were put into the sauna in sacks or thick piles, and the stove was heated up right away. Steam was created by throwing water on the stones of the stove, akin to giving the grains a sauna bath. In fact, some people had a sauna themselves while malting. This step of wet heat was called sweetening, and it was continued until the malt tasted sweet. The sweetening was followed by drying, in which the malt was spread out thinly, maintaining dry heat. Often sweetening took one day, followed by a day of drying.

Because the craft of sweetening was forgotten half a century ago, it is difficult to say what kind of malt and ale it produced. My educated guess is that the sweetening produced a kind of caramel malt with starches mostly converted to sugars. The reasoning behind this claim is rather technical, so bear with me, or skip the next two paragraphs.

When commercial caramel malt is produced in the kiln, a thick layer of wet germinated grains is first heated to 140 to 176°F (60 to 80°C), which converts the starch inside the kernels into sugar. The malt is then dried at higher temperatures, up to 250°F (121°C). In this process, the interior of the malt bed retains moisture better, resulting in candy-like caramel flavors, while malt closer to the surface dries more quickly, picking up flavors of bread crust.

Clearly those starch-conversion conditions were met by a steamy smoke sauna—the temperature range is actually a perfect match for having a sauna. But drying temperatures in the sauna probably did not reach 250°F (121°C), and they were more likely to be in the range of 176–230°F (80–110°C). With these lower drying temperatures, the flavor of sweetened farmhouse malt was probably more in the vein of baked bready notes rather than candy-like caramel.

In contrast, most caramel malt today is produced in rotated drum roasters where the final temperature rises above 350°F (177°C), giving a distinct candy-like caramel taste. Those conditions are far from those of smoke saunas, and of commercial malt kilns as well.

THE FINNISH SAUNA

Finland has five million people and more than two million saunas. The average Finn enjoys a sauna weekly. I can hardly think of anything more Finnish than the sauna. Modern saunas, whether heated by a wood fire or by electricity, do not generate smoke, but the smoke saunas of the olden days still haven't been forgotten. Today a smoke sauna is a special occasion that takes the bather almost shamanically into the days of yore.

Søndergård Såinnhus is a traditional malt house in Stjørdal, Norway, that is still in active use. The malting is operated by a group of farmhouse homebrewers, and one session yields 350 pounds (160 kilograms) of malt. The malt rests on perforated planks. Beneath these, fire generates heat and air flow, which together dry the malt. The resulting malt and ale are immensely smoky—and very tasty for those who like the taste of smoke. MIKA LAITINEN

Farmers malted both barley and rye with these two methods, but the sweetening was more typical for rye. In fact, sahti folks still often refer to rye malt as "the sweets" (*imelät*). Also, in the old ethnological surveys, some brewers mentioned that rye malt makes sahti sweeter, while barley malt makes it stronger in alcohol. Perhaps it was the sweetening that made sahti less fermentable, and hence sweeter and less intoxicating.

Another common conception among sahti folks is that rye produces a darker color than barley. Pale rye malt is indeed slightly darker than pale barley malt, but apparently a greater distinction was created by the differences in malting. Surveys indicate that sweetening produced darker malt than dry ascending heating, and often a darker quality was one of the aims in sweetening. Nevertheless, farmhouse maltsters wanted to avoid roasting the malt, and they had other methods for obtaining that

In 2001, the sahti folks of Isojoki established Sahtiopisto, or the Sahti Academy, which provides malting and brewing facilities for members. Many of the group members malt and brew with their own grains. The photo on the left shows a steeping tank and germination frames. Malt is dried by blowing hot air through the grain bed with the equipment shown on the right. The dryer has an optional smoking unit that can be used to introduce smoke into the stream, mimicking the old days.

sought-after reddish-brown color. For example, small amounts of grain were roasted in a pan-like coffee roaster.

Elsewhere in the Nordic region, traditional brewers have also used buildings known as *kjølne, kölna,* and *såinnhus* that are dedicated to drying malt. These structures are built around a wood-fired kiln and a shallow platform for grain. The drying principle is simple and effective: hot smoke from the kiln is channeled through the malt bed. Maltings of this type are still used in parts of Norway, especially in the municipality of Stjørdal, near Trondheim. As far as I know, Finnish farmhouse brewers haven't used this kind of malting.

The Norwegians have had smoke saunas as well, but they quit bathing in them a long time ago. Even if having a sauna was forgotten, the smoke saunas were retained for malting, and a few Norwegian farmhouse brewers still malt in them.

I have tasted stjørdalsøl, the Norwegian farmhouse ale made from traditionally kilned barley malt, and I could recognize that huge smoke aroma from yards away. Surely the Finnish farmhouse malt was smoky too, but I'm pretty sure that the smokiness was milder, because the smoke wasn't flowing through the grain bed. Some traditional Finnish food products, such as cured pork or riihi-dried rye (unmalted), are still made in a smoke sauna or riihi, and they tend to have a mild to moderate smoke aroma.

The flavor and intensity of the smoke depends on the fuel too. Nordic maltsters have usually favored alderwood, which produces softer smoke than, for example, beech or oak. In Gotland, some farmhouse maltsters have used birch, which conveys a pungent smokiness.

In the past, malt was dried with smokeless techniques too, but usually these are applied on a smaller scale and less efficient for colder climates. For example, in the Nordic region malt has been dried on hot stone slabs and in baking ovens. In northern climates, sun-drying is not the most prominent method, but it has been practiced occasionally in Finland and Norway nonetheless, and it used to be fairly common in the farmhouse breweries of Lithuania. Sun-drying is said to produce very pale malt with a cucumber-like green malt character.

Commercial Malt

For decades now, Viking Sahti Malt, sold by Viking Malt, has been the mainstay of sahti brewers. Viking Malt is a Nordic malting company with several maltings in northern Europe, and its Sahti Malt is produced in the maltings of Lahti, Finland, within the sahti heartland. Also, the barley for this malt is grown in the surrounding areas, within or at least near the traditional sahti regions.

Viking Sahti Malt is a proprietary blend containing principally Pilsner malt and smaller amounts of specialty malts. Viking Malt is secretive about exactly what specialty malts go into the blend, and it has

Germinating malt at Viking Malt in Lahti, Finland.

been speculated that this blend contains caramel malts. However, from inspecting the malt I see no signs of caramelized sugars, and I suspect the presence of other highly kilned dark malts more. The blend produces a golden- to copper-colored sahti if used on its own. (The color unit of Sahti Malt is around 5 to 10 EBC, or 2.5 to 4°L. The malt color unit EBC is used by European maltsters and brewers, while the unit Lovibond, expressed as °L, is more common in North America.)

It is unclear when Sahti Malt was first produced, but the malt house in Lahti was founded in 1934, for what was then part of the distillery and yeast factory Lahden Polttimo. The oldest surviving sales records for this malt are from the 1950s, and according to ethnographic surveys, this is the decade when commercial malt began replacing farmhouse malt. How the company arrived at this blend has been lost in the mists of history, but discussion with the malt house staff left me with the impression that the aim was to design malt best suited to sahti, rather than to mimic the old farmhouse malt.

Wide availability and ease of use add to the popularity of Sahti Malt. In the sahti heartland, this blend is sold precrushed in grocery stores. In 2014 Viking Malt revamped its packaging line, and Sahti Malt moved from 44-pound (20-kilogram) sacks to sacks containing 55 pounds (25 kilograms) each. This led to surprising recipe changes, since traditional brewers often measure their malt by sackful and not by weight. One renowned brewer, for example, simply kept brewing the same volume of sahti from two sacks of malt, despite the 25 percent increase in malt weight.

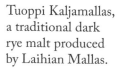
Tuoppi Kaljamallas, a traditional dark rye malt produced by Laihian Mallas.

A minority of sahti brewers use other commercial malt instead of Sahti Malt. Pilsner, Vienna, and Munich malts are the most popular additions, and, as far as I'm concerned, these are just as good a choice. In Estonia, Pilsner malt seems to be the favorite among the koduõlu brewers.

Another very popular addition to sahti is the dark roasted rye malt called Tuoppi Kaljamallas, from the Finnish malt house Laihian Mallas. While intended for brewing traditional Finnish small beer (kalja), it appears also in most sahtis today. This addition probably honors the old tradition of roasting grains for color. Kaljamallas has a chestnut color and it produces color similar to that of dark caramel malt (its color value is around 180 EBC or 70°L). Those who use it only for color add around 5 percent to impart a reddish-brown hue.

Kaljamallas has a distinct flavor that is somewhat difficult to describe. The traditional Finnish dessert *mämmi*, a sweet pudding made from malted and unmalted rye, would be a perfect descriptor, but few people outside Finland have tasted this rustic dessert. Perhaps the crusts of dark rye bread would afford the second-best description. Brewers who are fond of that taste and a dark brown color use around 10 percent of this malt. The higher percentage of dark malt is often balanced by a sweeter taste, as found in the acclaimed sahti areas of Padasjoki and Lammi.

Some brewers feel that Kaljamallas gives a sharp taste so avoid using it altogether. They either brew paler yellow-orangey sahti or use caramel barley malt for a reddish-brown color. Usually the caramel malt is a drum-roasted version from Viking Malt. Drum roasting is further from the tradition, but at levels of 5 to 10 percent the caramel malt can hardly be detected in the taste.

Grain Quantities and Alcohol Content

Today brewers typically make 1 to 1.5 quarts of sahti from 1 pound of grains (2 to 3 liters from a kilogram). This yields a heady and full-bodied brew.

It seems that these ratios have remained fairly similar for the last hundred years, which is as far back as Finnish ethnographers' records of farmhouse brewing extend. Home-malted grains from heirloom grain varieties likely gave less extract, but even when that is taken into account, sahti has been rich and potent at least throughout its recorded history.

— 9 —

Yeast

That Mysterious Touch in Liquid Lore

MODERN BREWER'S YEAST has been purified and cultured in a laboratory to labor tirelessly and efficiently. Also, today's brewers treat their yeast in a very sophisticated manner in order to avoid alien bacteria. Compared to that, traditional farmhouse yeast-handling methods sound like something out of a fairy tale: storing the house yeast on a dried birch whisk, crumbling the yeast with one's bare hands, and fermenting with a yeast that starts off with bacteria in the mix. How on earth could that make good beer?

That is the beauty of brewing history. The folk who came before us figured out brewing practices that work, by trial and error—methods that we never could have guessed at even with all our advanced knowledge of brewing science. Yeast and fermentation are certainly the most mysterious part of liquid lore.

Where the Yeast Came From

The late nineteenth century brought a pivotal moment in brewing. Louis Pasteur discovered that yeast is a living microorganism causing alcoholic fermentation. Emil Christian Hansen developed methods for isolating and using pure yeast strains. Commercial baker's yeast entered the market. Yet centuries before Pasteur, both domestic and commercial brewers knew the concept of yeast and had their domesticated house yeasts.

Where did this yeast originate, and how old is it? Nobody knows. It has been cultured with traditional methods at a Norwegian farmhouse brewery for as long as anybody remembers. MIKA LAITINEN

Nature hosts an abundance of yeast, especially close to sugar sources—such as the surface of fruits, berries, and plants. The fermentation of sugary liquid isn't the hard part. It's difficult to prevent, and the real challenge is to suppress the unwanted microbes, such as lactic and acetic acid bacteria.

The most archaic way of fermenting is just to wait for it to happen. Airborne and resident wild yeasts and bacteria eventually ferment the liquid into beer, but souring too is inevitable. This so-called spontaneous fermentation is how sharply acidic Belgian lambics are still made today. Also some low-alcohol farmhouse beers in eastern Finland were fermented in this way as recently as the first half of the twentieth century. Yet I haven't found a single reference indicating that sahti or its cousins elsewhere in the Nordic and Baltic areas were fermented spontaneously. Instead, they have relied on cultivated yeasts and on practices that can keep souring bacteria at bay.

Early on, brewers noticed that fermentation goes better if something from the previous batch of beer is transferred to the new batch. Through trial and error they found practices that supported good fermentation and suppressed souring. Eventually this led to domesticated strains of "house yeast," which were reused from batch to batch. Similar yeast domestication occurred in baking, and in some houses the strains for baking and brewing were the same.

As discussed in the chapter on history, we don't know when exactly the brewing yeasts were domesticated, but the first written description of brewing sahti, from 1780, clearly refers to reliance on yeast and describes methods to avoid sourness.

In most cases, its guardians don't know how their heirloom yeast got started, and if something is said about the origin, it usually sounds like pure legend: "My grandfather found the yeast in a forest." Finnish folk wisdom has it that if yeast is not available, boar's saliva will get fermentation started, and that a rutting boar would yield the briskest fermenting. I thought this was a legend until I found an ethnographic monograph from 1948 that actually describes the practice of collecting saliva in detail.

Farmhouse Yeast

There was a whole cornucopia of farmhouse methods for harvesting and maintaining the house yeasts. In some houses, the froth from fermenta-

Dried flakes of a traditional farmhouse yeast, a kveik from Hornindal, Norway. This yeast has never been handled in accordance with laboratory methods or modern brewing science, yet it produces extremely tasty beer. On a brew day, the yeast is "awakened" in a small amount of wort, and within a few hours it is ready for action. MIKA LAITINEN

tion was skimmed off the top and stored in a piece of cloth. Sometimes top or bottom sludge was scraped into a birch whisk, which was then dried. Pieces of wood, juniper twigs, or hop cones were dropped into the fermenting vessel and later collected and dried. In Finland the pieces of wood were often in simple shapes like cubes, but in Scandinavia brewers also used logs or rings that were carefully crafted to maximize surface area and yeast collection. A relatively new method was to collect the material at the bottom of the vessel into a glass bottle for storage in a well.

Although yeast was collected only from good batches, occasionally the house strain went sour or got lost. A replacement was sought from a neighbor, and often this led to collective strains typical of certain geographical areas.

Although house yeasts had been used for sahti in the early twentieth century, commercial baker's yeast superseded the Finnish house strains by the 1950s, and literature from the 1960s generally refers to the house yeasts as already a thing of the past. Finnish bakers have held on to their heirloom yeasts better: hundreds of households and commercial bakeries still leaven their rye bread with a traditional generations-old sourdough starter.

Traditional farmhouse yeasts have survived in some remote locations in Norway, Lithuania, Latvia, and Russia, as discovered by Lars Marius Garshol. Typically these heirloom treasures have been passed down through the family longer than anybody remembers, and their age and origin are usually unknown. The yeasts are maintained and used with a great deal of tried-and-true folk wisdom, completely devoid of modern laboratory work or brewing science. These yeasts are unique and should be treated as national treasures! The folk wisdom surrounding their use echoes that of old-time Finland, and these traditions give a good sense of what sahti brewers have lost.

Microbiologists have started analyzing farmhouse yeasts and storing them in yeast banks. This has led to several recent discoveries about the qualities of Norwegian yeasts, which I will summarize below. This helps to paint a more general picture. Baltic and Russian farmhouse yeasts have been analyzed far less than their Norwegian cousins, but they seem to share many of the traits uncovered.

Norwegian farmhouse brewers have several names for their house yeasts, which are variously known as *kveik*, *gjær*, *gjest*, and *barm*, but recently they have become internationally known as kveik. I will use this term throughout the book.

Actually most kveiks are mixtures of microbes, typically containing three to seven individual yeast strains. Some kveiks include souring bacteria also, but surprisingly many of the kveiks analyzed have been completely free of bacteria—the yeasts had overthrown them. The mixture seems to ferment better than any single strain extracted from the mix. One farmhouse brewer who provided his kveik for analysis and got it back purified to a single yeast strain ended up disappointed. He didn't like how this yeast fermented, so he reverted to his original kveik.

So far the most extensive kveik study has been done by microbiologist Richard Preiss and his colleagues. They analyzed nine kveiks from Norway and one traditional farmhouse yeast from Lithuania. Several commercial ale yeasts from White Labs were used as a reference.

The analysis revealed most yeast strains in kveiks to be of the same species as standard brewer's ale yeast, *Saccharomyces cerevisiae*. This result is far from trivial, since nature has plenty of other species that can ferment beer wort well—yet more proof of the intimate symbiosis of *S. cerevisiae* with humankind. However, the DNA of kveiks showed remarkable differences from all the commercial ale yeasts. Furthermore, the DNA analysis clustered kveiks into two separate groups that match the geography of Norway: when Garshol mapped these kveiks, he noticed that the two groups are separated by mountains and glaciers.

Farmhouse brewers didn't have efficient wort-cooling devices, so they wanted to add yeast as soon as the wort had cooled to temperatures at which yeast can work. They also wanted the yeast to work quickly and drop out of solution as soon as the work was done. The study by Preiss and colleagues confirmed that kveiks do this more efficiently than normal brewer's yeast. They can grow and ferment even at above 104°F (40°C). The fermentation is furious, and the ale is relatively clear of yeast two or three days from brewing. Kveiks tolerate high levels of alcohol as well, typically 13 to 16 percent.

An ale fermented with kveik has a distinct fruity flavor of its own. However, this isn't pungent, especially when one considers that these yeasts like to ferment at 86 to 104°F (30 to 40°C), where most yeasts become highly expressive. Center stage is granted to sweet maltiness.

Somewhat surprisingly, kveiks do not usually produce the spicy and clovey phenolic flavors typical of Belgian farmhouse yeasts and Finnish baker's yeast. In the Preiss study, none of the kveiks had this habit. A phenolic taste is typical for wild yeasts, and usually a yeast lacking this trait has been selectively bred—the brewer preferred the ale without tastes of clove so selected yeast accordingly.

I have played with several kveiks in my home brewery and tasted a few ales fermented with them in Norway. The kveik from Voss, known as Sigmund's kveik, offered intriguing fruitiness reminiscent of gummy candies. A Hornindal-area kveik yielded flavors of red berries and citrus fruits. Sahti fermented with kveik tastes remarkably different from what Finnish baker's yeast creates, but I see no reason to suspect that the Finnish farmhouse yeasts were different from kveiks.

In addition, I tested one traditional Lithuanian farmhouse yeast that rendered extravagant flavors of toffee, butter, and popcorn. In most modern beers a butter flavor (diacetyl) is a flaw, but I did not find the taste unpleasant, and I can imagine that in olden times, before candies and lemonade, sweet toffeeish ale would have been a real hit.

I have concluded also that the traditional ways of handling the yeast made their own contribution to the flavor. For instance, some traditional ales have a mushroomy broth-like taste that may be attributable to breakdown of yeast cells (autolysis). Again, this would be a fault according to modern brewing science, but if you can overlook that, you might be delighted with the exuberant umami flavors.

Today kveiks are available to both commercial brewers and homebrewers through yeast companies. They have already been employed for all kinds of craft beer, IPAs and beyond. I find great potential in kveiks as an interesting tool for craft brewers far outside the realm of traditional ales, but I do think they shine best in smooth-drinking malty ales, or in a microbe medley for sour ales.

Commercial Yeast

Commercial baker's yeast is of the same species as ale yeast (*S. cerevisiae*), but it has been selected and bred for different purposes. Baker's yeast

Fresh compressed baker's yeast produced by Suomen Hiiva has been the mainstay of sahti brewers for decades. Many attributes associated with the essence of sahti, such as a hefty banana aroma, are actually produced by this yeast. MIKA LAITINEN

leavens bread efficiently, while brewer's yeast effectively ferments various malt sugars, produces good-tasting beer, and flocculates conveniently to the bottom after fermentation. Also, the hygiene requirements differ between baking and brewing. A small amount of lactic bacteria does no harm in baking but can render beer undrinkable.

Today Suomen Hiiva is the only Finnish producer of baker's yeast, and its main product for consumers is a 1.8-ounce (50-gram) package of fresh compressed baker's yeast. For most sahti brewers, this is the classic sahti yeast.

The origins of Suomen Hiiva can be traced back to the inception of commercial yeast production, in the 1880s, albeit through several changes in ownership, production methods, and factory locations. The plant manager assured me that the strain has been the same for at least a few decades, and I haven't heard or read about changes in the flavors of fermentation.

Since 1995 this yeast has been produced in Lahti, Finland. The factory churns out tens of millions of pounds of baker's yeast each year, enough to supply the whole of Finland. Coincidentally, the yeast factory and the malt house producing Sahti Malt are neighbors, because both were part of the Polttimo Group in the 1990s. In 2007 this business group sold Suomen Hiiva to the international Lallemand Inc., but the yeast production remained in Lahti.

A few sahti brewers use dried baker's yeast, although in 2018 none are produced in Finland. The foreign origin of baker's yeast does not contravene the EU appellation for sahti, and it is not an issue for the brewers either. Although Suomen Hiiva's fresh compressed yeast is somewhat temperamental to brew with, most brewers just prefer its character.

Suomen Hiiva produces this compressed yeast from a single strain in a highly controlled manner. When producing millions of pounds, one cannot expect totally bacteria-free yeast. The company's standard is one lactic bacterium to ten thousand yeast cells. The yeast is likely to pick up more of these bacteria in the grocery store, where it is sold paper-wrapped alongside dairy products.

Indeed, sahti made with baker's yeast usually turns sour at some point, irrespective of the sanitation practices employed. Farmhouse breweries have many potential sources of souring bacteria, but I believe that the bacteria within the baker's yeast are the main contributor. I have fermented unboiled sahti wort many times with pure brewer's yeast, and those ales have never soured.

German wheat beer (weizen) yeast produces a flavor somewhat similar to the effects of Suomen Hiiva's fresh compressed yeast, but brewer's yeast is considered an inauthentic ingredient in sahti, and against the Traditional Speciality Guaranteed appellation. Admittedly, today's single-strain brewer's yeast is a highly bred outcome of science, and thereby distinct from the farmhouse cultures.

Sahti has been fermented with baker's yeasts for more than a century, and this practice has become a tradition in its own right. Use of baker's yeast has the side effect of forcing brewers to follow the traditional fermentation and storage techniques originally developed to combat souring bacteria. It does make sahti difficult to store, transport, and sell, but that is part of the tradition. All in all, baker's yeast captures many aspects of the original farmhouse cultures, even though the latest laboratory studies have shown that traditional farmhouse yeasts are clearly different from commercial baker's yeast.

In other Nordic and Baltic farmhouse ales, the distinction maintained between baker's and brewer's yeast is less sharp. For example, in Estonia koduõlu brewers unapologetically use both yeast types.

How Commercial Yeast Changed Farmhouse Brewing

Old stories reveal only a little of how sahti folks reacted to the arrival of commercial yeast. Naturally, the change was not welcomed by everyone, and many pined for the lost house strains. Some complained that commercial baker's yeast ferments too quickly—the brewers did not want fermentation to halt right away, because slow secondary fermentation protects against souring.

People who haven't seen the traditional yeast-handling techniques or tasted ales brewed with them often assume that commercial baker's yeast improved the ale's quality. After all, how could farmers without any professional training or understanding of brewing science have maintained and reused clean yeast for generations? This is indeed incredible: the recent laboratory analyses of kveiks have shown that farmhouse yeasts can be cleaner of bacteria than baker's yeast is. There is no indication that sahti became cleaner or tastier when farmers switched to commercial yeast.

From my own experience, I can state that the traditional farmhouse practices for handling yeast require a great deal of consistency. In my testing of the traditional house cultures and methods for maintaining them, more than once my ales have gone sour. If a traditional yeast is not handled in strict accordance with what folklore dictates, the ale and the whole yeast culture could be ruined. A Norwegian brewer using kveik reckoned that it would be difficult to keep kveik alive without help from other brewers. The great effort and uncertainties surrounding house yeasts probably were the main reasons for abandoning them.

The transition to a single strain of yeast used by nearly every brewer surely homogenized the flavors of sahti, though Suomen Hiiva's yeast can yield surprisingly different flavors that depend on the brewer. In such a fresh and malt-oriented beer as sahti, the loss of character and diversity was not necessarily huge, but I can't help but wonder what sahti would be like if Finnish farmhouse yeasts had survived.

Reviving the House Cultures

By following what the farmhouse brewers have been doing, we can actually regenerate house yeasts. The first thing we need is a functional first generation of yeast, which we begin to recycle from batch to batch. The seed yeast can be captured from the wild, picked from sourdough starters, or resurrected from old beer residues. With traditional yeast-handling practices and a bit of luck, the yeast will eventually adapt to its environment and grow into a culture that performs well in the brewhouse. This is a lot of work, but that's how farmhouse yeasts got started.

To test the workability of this idea, in 2015 I cultivated my own "kveik" from an old Finnish sourdough starter. I pitched a spoonful of the porridge-like starter into hopped wort. Fermentation began promptly but stopped at 2 percent ABV. The test seemed a failure at first, but after a week another strain took over and fermented the wort to completion. I collected the residual yeast and started repitching the yeast from batch to batch. With the third generation of this yeast, I brewed sahti for the Finnish National Sahti Competition. The brew didn't place in the finals, but people generally liked the taste and considered it authentic. I have

An old sourdough starter from which brewing yeast has been harvested. MIKA LAITINEN

nurtured this yeast ever since with only farmhouse methods. So far, one batch has gone sour from acetic bacteria, but luckily I had an older backup to regenerate the yeast.

This yeast ferments very dry and can tolerate high alcohol levels. It produces extremely little fruitiness or spiciness in the aroma (esters and phenols). It has a bad habit of producing a taste of sharp alcohol, but perhaps I will be able to train out that behavior. I have sent the sourdough starter to Norway, where it was cultured for research purposes at the Norwegian University of Science and Technology. The yeast was used as a reference yeast in Truls Rasmussen's master's thesis project on Norwegian farmhouse yeasts. According to genetic analysis, the yeast is of the species *Candida humilis*, which is very unusual for brewing yeasts but entirely typical for sourdough starters. While my ongoing experiment with this yeast has shown its viability, we should remember that although the starter I used is at least several decades old, its actual link to brewing is unknown.

Since there are homes in Finland that used the same house strain for baking and brewing before the 1950s, it is possible that some old sourdough starters in the sahti districts still contain old brewing yeast. Perhaps traditional brewing strains are still lurking in them, waiting to be restored to their original brewing work.

– 10 –

Brewing Herbs

Preserving, Filtering, and Flavoring Too

IT SEEMS THAT NORDIC AND BALTIC farmhouse brewers have liked the taste of malt above all else. They have seasoned their ales with juniper, hops, and a few other plants, but the flavor of these plants has been very mild in most brews of this sort I have tasted. Even the word *seasoning* might be misleading. Juniper and hops might have originally ended up in northern farmhouse ales because of their practical effects as preservatives and filtering aids. This applies to brews of the past in general: many beer ingredients that we today think of as mere flavorings played a more fundamental role in ancient brews.

Before hops, the ancient ale additives were often gathered from the wild. Among them was juniper, which would be difficult to cultivate. In contrast, hops lend themselves well to cultivation and large-scale brewing. When hops entered the scene, they hence brought great change and paved the way for modern large brewing volumes. However, at rural Nordic farmhouse breweries, hops have never been able to outcompete juniper.

Juniper

Common juniper (*Juniperus communis*) is a hardy conifer that grows widely in the Northern Hemisphere around the world. Wherever it is found, indigenous peoples have utilized it in a versatile manner for millennia. It has been valued as a folk medicine, cleaning agent, and flavoring for foods and drinks, while also providing wood for crafting small vessels and utensils. For traditional farmhouse brewers, juniper has been as much

Before hops, juniper was the most important brewing herb in the Nordic region.

133

a cleaning agent and filtering aid as a flavoring. It even seems that for some brewers its refreshing flavor is merely a side effect.

Unlike gin distillers, the northern farmhouse brewers use the branches of the tree, not just its berries. These branches make an exceptionally handy brewing ingredient since they can be collected at any time of the year, usually from the brewer's backyard or a nearby forest. They can go straight from tree to brew.

The cleaning action comes from the *juniper infusion* or *juniper water*, made by infusing branches in hot or boiling water for at least an hour. Sahti folks use this infusion as a disinfectant, rinsing all their wooden vessels with it. In fact, juniper berries and needles have been shown to possess antimicrobial properties, though the scientific research has concentrated on pathogens rather than on beer-spoilage bacteria. Juniper branches release resins into the hot water, creating a durable coating on the surfaces it touches. It is likely that this resin layer also reduces the number of bacteria harbored by the wooden vessels.

Some Nordic and Baltic farmhouse brewers use juniper infusion also for their brew water, either the full volume or a portion of it. This can add considerable flavor, but the intensity varies greatly, depending on the proportion of infusion and the quantity of branches in it.

Another major use of juniper branches is to lay them at the bottom of the lautering vessel, to act as a strainer when the wort is draining out from the mash. The wort picks up some flavors when it flows through the bed of juniper branches, but usually that added flavor will not be overpowering no matter how many branches there are. Today most sahti lautering vessels would work fine without the juniper filter, but many brewers stack the branches on the bottom of the lauter tun anyway for the sake of tradition and flavor.

Juniper branches have three flavor sources: the needles, berries, and wood. So it is only natural that the flavor imparted by branches differs clearly from that provided by berries alone. The branches have a more coniferous taste. Both the needles and the berries are rich in essential oils, especially in alpha-pinene, which imparts piney and herbal flavors. Some brewers like the flavor effect of the wood as well and prefer to include thicker, woodier branches for this reason.

Brewers in Finland and Estonia generally prefer a soft and gentle juniper flavor, while in Gotland and parts of Norway the juniper char-

On the eve of a brew day, sahti master Hannu Sirén harvests some juniper branches from his backyard.

acter can sometimes be even pungent. Those who strive for a more pronounced juniper flavor often use juniper infusion for all their brew water.

Juniper varies widely in character, and its traits depend hugely on the location and species. In sahti areas, the plant is always *J. communis* of the subspecies *communis*. What is referred to as juniper elsewhere can be very different in appearance and flavor. Even the subspecies can make a big difference.

In 2012 a renowned brewmaster and sahti brewer, Markku Pulliainen from Malmgård Brewery, obtained concrete proof of this diversity. He was visiting Philadelphia to brew a collaboration beer with Dock Street Brewery, an authentic sahti crafted just as is done in Finland. Pulliainen sent Finnish baker's yeast by mail and carried Finnish rye malt in his suitcase. In Philadelphia he and the Dock Street partners went to a local arboretum to pick juniper branches. When Pulliainen saw the tree, he was stunned. The species was indeed *J. communis*, but it neither looked nor tasted like Finnish juniper. According to Pulliainen, the branches had a perfumed aroma, unlike the refreshing scent of Finnish forests.

Besides the species and subspecies, many other factors affect the flavor. Juniper has separate male and female plants, and berries grow only on the female ones. Biologist Minna-Maarit Kytöviita informed me that needles of the female plants have more flavor compounds. Some sahti brewers have traditionally favored branches that sport numerous berries, but the reason hence might not lie in the berry itself. Perhaps sahti folks have intuitively recognized that the branches with berries are more flavorful. In addition, the age of the tree, the soil, and the amount of sunlight all affect the flavor. The substantial differences possible become clear when one remembers that juniper trees can be hundreds of years old.

Although sahti is generally seen as a juniper ale, some contemporary versions are brewed without the plant. In 2006 Heikki Riutta from Sysmä took part in the National Sahti Competition with a juniper-less sahti: on brew day he simply hadn't had time to collect branches. He won the competition, and the judges described his sahti as full-bodied and junipery—Finnish baker's yeast produces spiciness that can easily overlap with juniper flavor for the drinker. Riutta hasn't used juniper since.

Juniper grows in Lithuania also, but it is not commonly used in the local farmhouse ales. While touring Lithuania, Lars Marius Garshol met a farmhouse brewer who makes an infusion from birch twigs for cleaning. Another brewer spoke of how in his family the lauter tun filter had been formed from raspberry canes instead of juniper branches.

Hops

Some people find it difficult to believe that hops grow as far north as Finland, Sweden, and Norway. Even a recent book on hops states that these sensitive-seeming plants grow between latitudes of 30° and 52°. However, I can attest that *landrace hops* (the term for a region's traditional local varieties) are growing in my garden, at a latitude of 62°, and I'm not the only one. Some Finns have reported old hop cultivars at 66°N, near the Arctic Circle.

Hop cultivation began surprisingly early in Nordic climes. The Vikings had hop gardens before AD 1000, though we don't know whether these were kept for ale. In the past, hops have been grown for several purposes, including dyeing and rope-making. As far as use in beer goes, laws in the fifteenth century required Finnish and Swedish farmers to grow hops, obviously for brewing purposes. While these farmers paid taxes in hops, written sources do not reveal whether they used hops themselves. Either way, hops gradually became commonplace in the Finnish countryside, but in the nine-teenth century commercial Finnish breweries switched to imported hops, and hop farming was largely forgotten. As of 2018, no Finnish hops are sold. Nevertheless, hop bines are still a typical sight around the country's farmsteads. If a sahti brewer uses hops, they are often homegrown.

The origin of Finnish hops remains a mystery. In the 2010s, research-ers analyzed dozens of Finnish landrace hops and found them to be genetically unrelated to commercial European hops. Many sources claim that hops are native to Finland, and they do appear in the wild here. However, so far all "wild" hops analyzed have been genetically related to nearby cultivated hops and appear to be strays. Those who have brewed with Finnish hops have reported low bitterness and mild aromas, with herbal and grassy qualities, sometimes reminiscent of birch leaves.

Given how exposed Finnish farmers have been to hops, they have used them surprisingly little. In the course of recorded history, the hop character of sahti has ranged from mild to none. The amounts and hop-ping methods described in ethnographic works are extremely varied, and it is impossible to tell whether the variation is by region, time-based, or brewer-specific. Adding confusion, the traditional quantities of hops are usually expressed rather imprecisely in handfuls.

In the first written description of brewing sahti, the material from 1780, the brewer uses a handful of hops for each *kappe* of malt, which

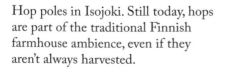

Hop poles in Isojoki. Still today, hops are part of the traditional Finnish farmhouse ambience, even if they aren't always harvested.

in modern units is a handful for 5.6 pounds (2.5 kilograms) of malt. The brewer boils the hops in a small amount of water for an hour and a half, then dumps the water, including the hop cones, into the wort. With Finnish heirloom hops, this probably did not yield a bitter sahti, but surprisingly this amount is much greater than in any other documentation of traditional sahti.

This kind of hop infusion has been a common way of adding hops among Nordic and Baltic farmhouse brewers. The method is particularly handy for brewers who don't boil their wort. Some brewers add the infusion with hop cones, while others strain away the cones. Without boiling, hops can also be added to the fermenter along with yeast, in a practice somewhat similar to modern dry hopping. If hop cones end up in the fermenter, the brewer typically strains them out when transferring the sahti to storage vessels. In the past, some sahti brewers dried the strained-out hops and used them as a vehicle for adding yeast to the next batch.

From twentieth-century ethnographic records, it is apparent that many sahti brewers wanted to benefit from the preservative effects of hops but disliked their bitterness. Finnish folk wisdom may even advise first reducing the bitterness by simmering the hops in hot water and then adding merely the hop cones to the sahti, discarding the liquid. Today's science tells us that this is counterproductive, since the preservative qualities are found mostly in the bitter compounds of boiled hops, dissolved in the liquid.

Fewer than half of today's sahti brewers use hops, and the rest use so little hopping that it barely contributes to flavor or preservation. Although hops are not untraditional for sahti, I have concluded that the lack of hop flavors and bitterness is part of the unique nature of sahti and an authentic element carried over from times before hopped beers.

Other Ingredients

Through the ages, nearly every herb, spice, and sugar source seems to have found its way into beer. Therefore it is surprising that sahti brewers seem to have trusted almost solely in malted and unmalted grains, yeast, juniper, and hops. If other ingredients were used more than merely in passing, those habits of the past were forgotten several generations ago.

Isolated references mention such ingredients for sahti as bog myrtle and yarrow, but the texts do not reveal whether the use was just in

Bog myrtle was a popular choice for flavoring ale across medieval Europe, and occasionally it has been used in northern farmhouse ales. Paavo Pruul, from Estonia, replaces some of the hops with bog myrtle in his recipe for wintertime koduõlu.

one experiment or more general practice. Similar juniper-and-hops-centered simplicity prevails also in the farmhouse ales of Estonia, Norway, and Sweden. Lithuania seems to be more relaxed in this regard, showing greater variety, but even there a farmhouse ale with exotic ingredients such as raspberry canes or red clover seems to be the exception and specially created.

Honey is a traditional ingredient in gotlandsdricke, but I haven't found any evidence of equivalent use in sahti. Neither is honey even compatible with the appellation of sahti. Finns have a history of using birch sap very creatively, and likely it has sometimes ended up in sahti, though a more typical drink using it is so-called *sap beer* (*mahlakalja*), basically a fermented birch sap.

The minerals in water affect the taste of beer, and geography-based differences in mineral composition have played a role in the evolution of the various beer styles. Most water sources in Finland offer a low mineral content, emphasizing a beer's rounded maltiness. Most Finns take high-quality water for granted, and sahti brewers rarely give much thought to it. With water quality being fairly uniform across the sahti districts, there is no indication that water has contributed to regional differences in sahti.

— II —

The Brewing Process

How Sahti Is Born

THE HARVEST HAD BEEN GENEROUS, and a feast was planned to honor the god of crops. Kylli, the lady of the farmhouse, played a central role in this feast. She was to brew sahti.

Kylli awoke before sunrise and continued without haste the work that had begun the night before. At a fireplace outside, she lit a fire and placed fist-sized stones into it. The wooden vats had already been wetted watertight, juniper branches had been soaking in hot water in a big wooden vat, and her man had crushed malt with a hand mill made of stone.

She poured the malt into a large wooden vat and moistened it with lukewarm water. Then she covered the vat and left for the morning's duties on the farm. After a while, she returned to pour more water over the malt. This time, the water was so hot that Kylli could barely draw her forefinger three times through the water in the bucket. The mash began to look like a thick porridge. Kylli left the mash to rest, and she went about her work in the farmhouse.

When Kylli came back, she lifted a hot stone from the fireplace with a big wooden fork and dropped the stone into a bucket of water, which then began to boil. She stirred briskly to avoid burning the bucket, then added boiling water to the mash. This made the mash easy to stir.

After letting the mash rest a third time, Kylli added several hot stones to it and stirred vigorously. The mash steamed and boiled fiercely. Now it was time to prepare a filtering vat, the kuurna, for draining the sweet wort

Today sahti is rarely brewed with this kind of brewing gear, but the brewing process is a relic of times when brewing vats were made of wood and heat was raised with hot stones.

141

from the mash. At the bottom of this vat, fashioned from a hollowed-out log, Kylli laid straw and juniper branches, and she then scooped the mash into the kuurna on top of the branches.

When the mashing vat was empty, Kylli cleaned it carefully and then rinsed it with hot juniper water. She drew the vat under the tapped lip of the kuurna, then released the flow of sweet barley juice into the vat. After a while, she began pouring hot juniper water over the bed of mash.

When the flow slowed down, she checked the thickness of the wort and stopped the flow when it began to feel thin to her finger. Her mother had warned many times against watering down sahti. She continued to rinse the grain bed with water, but this thinner liquor would be fermented separately and drunk before the feast. The youngsters gathered around the kuurna to taste the sweet malt juice.

The wort in the vat was left to cool. In the wee hours, when the wort was no warmer than her elbow, she stirred it with a birch whisk containing the "vigor" of fermentation from a previous batch. While stirring, she shouted, "The sun has risen! The moon has risen. When will *you* rise?" In the morning, the wort had become crowned with lively foam, and Kylli felt relieved. The next day, the foam calmed down, so she transferred the sahti to a wooden cask.

A diagram of the brewing process—the main ways of brewing the wort for sahti. Today the raw-ale approach is perhaps the most common, and boiled mash comes second. Most sahti brewers do not boil their wort as modern brewers do. While the text addresses only these three methods, farmhouse folk have used several hybrids also. For example, a portion of the wort may be drawn off for boiling and then poured back into the mash. MIKA LAITINEN

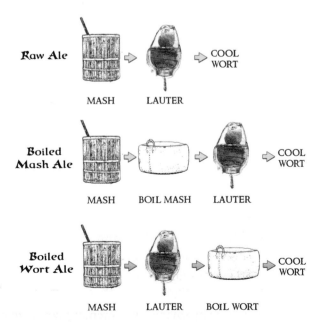

The ale matured four nights in the cask. At the feast, jolly villagers circulated a jug of ale until it couldn't be filled again—the cask was empty. They praised Kylli's brewing skills and temperate use of water.

That is my idea of how sahti was brewed in the mists of history. From archaeological findings, we know that the equipment in the story was typical for the Iron Age. From today's sahti traditions, we know that the brewing process in the story would have worked. These kinds of stories were not written down before 1780, so we don't know when exactly it all began.

Brewers' Gender

A frequently quoted fact is that *Kalevala*, the national epic of Finland, describes the creation of the world in two hundred verses, while four hundred are required to explain the origin of beer. In the twentieth rune, the first beer is brewed by female characters Osmotar, Kalevalatar, and Kapo while the manly figures Ahti, Kauko, and Lemminkäinen become intoxicated from the brew. In the old Nordic cultures, drinking is generally seen as men's affair, but the *Kalevala* does say that ale "puts smiles on women's lips, men in good spirits."

In *Historia de Gentibus Septentrionalibus* (*History of the Northern Peoples*), published in 1555, Olaus Magnus notes that "in the Nordic countries brewing and baking has been assigned exclusively to women, except in princes' courts, at aristocrats' houses, and for large gatherings." He largely attributes the high quality of northern ale to the meticulousness and cleanliness applied by women.

Before the twentieth century, brewing of sahti was almost solely the work of women, and a part of the household work that was taught to their daughters early on. The skills might have spread to new areas through marriages. After World War II, men got involved in the brewing of sahti, and today most of the brewers are men. In the renowned sahti district of Isojoki, it was explained to me that the men returning from the war were so thirsty for sahti that women got fed up with brewing, so men had to engage in the practice. Older brewers still remember being taught by their mothers or grandmothers.

Marja-Liisa Ylitalo, from Kärkölä, Finland, commented on the gender differences by saying, "For men, it takes a whole day to brew sahti and that's all they can do in a day. When womenfolk brew, they bake and take care of the kids and animals on the side." She was known to look after four children and four hundred pigs concurrently with brewing.

Also, in Sweden the making of gotlandsdricke used to be women's work, including the very laborious task of malting. In medieval England, domestic unhopped ales were brewed exclusively by women, and brewing shifted to being a man's profession in the late Middle Ages as hopped beer brewed on a larger scale became common.

In the Nordic and Baltic region, there have been exceptions to the pattern, at least in the last few centuries. In Estonia, farmhouse brewing has been men's work for generations, although the tradition of koduõlu is otherwise similar to that of making sahti. In the early twentieth century, Norway's farmhouse ales were brewed by both men and women.

Cleanliness

It takes courage to brew a beer with primitive techniques for big feasts— for example, to serve at weddings with hundreds of guests. In fact, the term "sahti master" has generally been reserved for a person who is trusted to brew good sahti for bigger parties and confident in doing so. These masters speak very emphatically about cleanliness, and, although their ideas

Making the juniper infusion in Hornindal, Norway. MIKA LAITINEN

of brewing hygiene do not always coincide with modern brewing science, they are highly skilled in ensuring good fermentation. Without proper cleaning of brewing vessels, fermentation becomes a game of chance, and it is likely that at some point souring bacteria will win.

The fundamental traditional cleaning method, still common today, is treating the brewing vessels with an old-time disinfectant: hot juniper infusion. The wooden vessels are first washed clean with water and then filled or rinsed with the infusion. Today, rinsing even plastic vessels and containers with juniper infusion is fairly common among sahti brewers.

An ancient trick is to fill a wooden vat with water and juniper branches, then drop hot stones into it, simultaneously creating the infusion and cleaning the vat. Nowadays, the juniper infusion is usually prepared in a cauldron or kettle.

Sometimes, a low-quality farmhouse ale can upset the stomach, and lack of hygiene is often blamed first. It is more likely for stomach-churning to be caused by large amounts of active yeast. This is a serious flaw in brewing but not related to hygiene.

Mashing

At modern breweries, mashing is usually completed in less than two hours, while traditional sahti mashing takes five to eight hours. In fact, sahti folks say, "Laziness is a virtue in a brewer," suggesting that mashing without haste yields superior ale.

Most sahti brewers today use modern commercial malt, but their brewing practices reflect a past of home-malted grains. Long mashing times certainly have been advantageous for homemade malt containing unevenly sprouted and dried grains. Shorter mashing could have led to poor extraction of the sugars and weaker sahti, which not only wastes grain but also frustrates the drinkers.

Because diluted ale may also follow from overly liberal use of water, there are several proverbs related to the desirable levels of laziness and strength of sahti. The brewer of a thin sahti might receive witty comments such as "you are too eager to carry water" or "your brewery is too close to a well."

That laziness does not seem to extend to waking up on a brew day, however. At 7:00 AM, most sahti masters are at least heating water, and some even wake up in the small hours to start brewing. After getting the grains wet, the brewer resumes the mashing calmly alongside other chores, without pressure for precise timing.

The main objective of the mashing, conversion of grain starch to sugars, occurs from 140 to 176°F (60 to 80°C); above 176°F (80°C) the enzymes responsible for conversion would begin to break down. It is far from obvious how the farmhouse brewers of yore managed the task without a thermometer.

Without a clue about enzymes, the old-time sahti brewers solved the problem by developing a mashing technique that takes the temperature of the mash slowly from hand-warm to very hot. Typically, the mash temperature and volume are raised by adding water three to six times with rests between the additions. Modern brewers call this method step mashing, while the sahti brewers speak of wetting the malt.

In the traditional wetting procedure, the water temperature increases with each step, starting with lukewarm and finishing with boiling water. Some brewers still use the ingenious old rules of thumb for determining water temperatures below the boiling point. For example, one might inspect the simmering of the water surface or test whether a finger can be drawn across the hot water.

In practice, every brewer seems to wet the malt in a slightly different way, with unique twists. To represent a simple, generic, and yet traditional mashing method, I developed the following procedure:

> First, wet the crushed grains with water slightly warmer than your hand. In the second step, use water so hot that you can barely touch it with your finger. The third, fourth, and fifth wetting are done with boiling water. After every water addition, stir thoroughly and let the mash rest for half an hour to an hour. In every step, use a volume ratio of 1 part water to 3.5 parts crushed grains. Modern brewers who weigh their grains should use 1 quart of water to 4 pounds of crushed grains, or 1 liter for every 2 kilograms.

This procedure raises the temperature slowly from hand-warm to above 158°F (70°C), provided that heat loss is small. To prevent heat loss between the water additions, the mashing vessel is usually covered, and

Lili Käär, from the Estonian island Hiiumaa, brews with a mash vat made in the early twentieth century from driftwood. In Estonia, farmhouse brewers typically are men, and Lili was the only female brewer I met there.

sometimes the vessel is also placed under a blanket. This method requires only a moderate amount of water (1.2 quarts of water for 1 pound of grains, or 2.5 liters for 1 kilogram), still fit for producing strong sahti.

In the first millennium AD, know-how in making large vats from staves of wood was commonplace in northern Europe. Metal vessels too were crafted then, but before the sixteenth century bigger cauldrons or kettles were far too expensive for common farming folk.

Therefore, a wooden vat is the most traditional vessel for mashing and still used by some farmhouse brewers in the Nordic and Baltic countries. The farmhouse brewers of the Estonian islands have especially impressive brewing gear—some of their actively used wooden tubs have already served several generations of brewers. Although still homebrewers, they use surprisingly large vessels: the typical batch size in the Estonian islands is 50 gallons (200 liters) of ale.

Wooden vats are very laborious to clean and maintain. Therefore, many of today's farmhouse brewers use stainless steel kettles or wood-fire-heated cauldrons. Large secondhand electric cooking kettles are fairly popular with sahti brewers too.

Sahti master Kari Harju at the cooperatively owned Sahtiopisto (Sahti Academy) in Isojoki. The brewing system includes a secondhand electric cooking kettle for mashing and stainless steel kuurna for lautering. This 80-gallon (300-liter) kettle yields 50 gallons (200 liters) of sahti.

Although most sahti brewers now use modern kettles and commercial malt, their brewing processes usually follow the ancient techniques, often learned by word of mouth from a family member. Some still find thermometers unnecessary, and most sahti brewers swear by a long mashing period of five to eight hours, citing tradition and superior taste. Some even claim that with a two-hour mash it isn't even sahti at all.

I was curious to know the effect of mashing time on taste and color, but it appeared that nobody had actually done side-by-side comparisons. So I performed a test of my own: the first sahti was mashed for ninety minutes, while the second was mashed for eight hours with a traditional five-step procedure. The longer mash time extracted the malt sugars slightly better, but the worts were equalized to the same gravity before fermentation (23°P).

The mashes were remarkably different in appearance, but the finished sahtis looked the same, without visible color differences. I expected differences in malty and cereal flavors, but the brews didn't diverge significantly in that respect.

Somewhat surprisingly, the main difference was in the fermentation. The sahti with the long mashing fermented to be slightly drier. The short-mash version, while being a touch sweeter, had slightly more alcohol sharpness. In a blind test with half a dozen people, the long-mash version was preferred by a 4–2 majority, but the quality difference was not regarded as significant.

This test was not highly scientific, but it demonstrated that the effect of mashing technique on taste is far from straightforward. The test worts were made from 94 percent barley malt and 6 percent rye malt. A higher proportion of malted rye or unmalted grains would likely have yielded more distinct differences.

Boiling

Let's return to the thesis of Carl Niclas Hellenius from 1780. Hellenius was originally from a traditional sahti district, Kärkölä, where the field work of the thesis likely took place. He observed a female brewer making sahti and documented the brewing process for the first time.

In the thesis, the brewer begins wetting the malt with cool water the night before the actual brew day, then continues the next morning with several additions of hot water. When the mash is wet enough that she can easily draw the mash paddle from rim to rim with one hand, the mash is left to rest and she begins to heat stones in a fireplace. Later, she drops red-hot stones into the mash and stirs vigorously, until the stones cannot burn the wooden tub. The mash is left to boil in a covered tub.

According to Hellenius, for each kappe of malt, one stone weighing six *marks* is needed. In modern units, this translates to around 5 pounds of stones for every 10 pounds of grain (5 kilograms of stones per 10 kilograms of grain). That is, to brew 25 gallons of sahti, around 40 pounds of stones is required (or 20 kilograms of stones for every 100 liters of sahti).

Hellenius wrote his thesis in the Age of Enlightenment, when it was customary to value science over tradition. Hence, he proposed reforms to the brewing practices. Hellenius stated that the flaws in the farmhouse brewing had been the main reason for the premature death of Finnish people. He regarded omitting the wort boil and boiling the mash with stones as among the greatest flaws.

Hellenius argued that the stones were detrimental to health because they boil the mash unevenly and crumble into the mash. Recently, commercial sahti brewery Hollolan Hirvi revived the tradition of brewing with stones, after which brewer Ilkka Sipilä mentioned that natural stones can be reused four or five times before they shatter from the heat shock. Inevitably, some granules do end up in the mash, but they are filtered out during the lautering step.

Hellenius also mentioned that the stones had an impact on flavor, which is easy to believe. Hollolan Hirvi brews its Kivisahti (literally, "stone sahti") with far fewer stones in the mash, yet the ale still has a delicate flavor of smoke, toffee, and caramel imparted by the mash burning and caramelizing on the surface of the stones.

Boiling the mash, either with stones or by heating a kettle, was commonly practiced over a hundred years ago. However, it's not always clear whether the boiling mentioned in the texts actually was preboil simmering, bringing to a boil, or longer boiling. In any case, adding even a small

Claws for handling hot stones, on display at the Linen and Sahti Museum in Lammi, Finland. Heating liquids with stones is an authentic Stone Age method used by indigenous peoples around the world.

number of red-hot stones to the mash is an impressive sight, causing the mash to steam, splash, and at least partly boil around the stones.

Although brewing with stones is rare today, I have been told that some domestic farmhouse brewers in Finland are still practicing the art. In addition to Hollolan Hirvi, a few traditional commercial breweries in Germany and Austria brew with stones, and the technique has been revived at some craft breweries, especially in the United States. However, the commercial breweries usually add the stones to the wort rather than the mash.

These days, some sahti brewers finish the mashing stage by simmering or boiling the mash in a kettle or cauldron, a practice likely originating from the stone boiling of yore. Brewers generally speak of boiling the mash, but many of them actually stop heating it as soon as grain husks and foam begin to rise to the surface. This may look like a gentle boil, but whenever I have checked these kinds of "boils" with a thermometer, the mash temperature has been in the range 176–194°F (80–90°C). Therefore, when sahti folks talk about boiling the mash, often it's best to think of simmering. Nevertheless, there are also brewers who perform an impressive rolling mash boil.

For some the length of the mash boil is more important than its vigor, and this may be connected with the type of sahti. Brewers in western Finland emphasize that in the crafting of sahti with a high rye content the mash should be boiled for at least half an hour. These rye sahtis seem to have toffee or caramel notes, which might be attributable to the long boil.

Boiling the mash can boost the extraction of malt sugars, but it can also leach residual starch from the grains after the enzymes have been destroyed, which can lead to starch in the beer. For this reason, the whole mash is never boiled at modern breweries. Some breweries perform what is known as decoction mashing, but that involves boiling only part of the mash, which makes it a distinctly different technique.

Instead of boiling the mash, modern brewers boil their wort with hops for one to two hours, as has been customary for commercial breweries since the late Middle Ages. In any case, Hellenius failed to convince the common Finns, and most sahti brewers still leave their wort unboiled, following the tradition originally formed when wooden vessels were commonly used.

Most sahtis are raw ales with a maximum temperature for both mash and wort probably in the range of 158–185°F (70–85°C). Some brewers do boil the wort to be on the safe side, but usually not for more than fifteen minutes. Apparently, this practice has filtered in from modern brewing, in which the wort *must* be boiled. A popular belief has it that boiling is needed to disinfect the wort, although practically all the bacteria die well below the boiling point. I regularly brew raw ales with a maximum temperature of 176°F (80°C), and the ones fermented with clean brewer's yeast have never gone sour. Admittedly, raw ales do go stale sooner, because of proteins and a few other compounds that are not precipitated by the wort boil.

Indeed, raw ales have an unmistakable protein-rich and nourishing character, while sahti from boiled wort may feel thinner and more "beery." The effect increases with boiling time, and after half an hour the difference is obvious. For ten to fifteen minutes, it is somewhere in between. Boiling the mash too precipitates proteins, but probably not to the same extent as a wort boil.

A sahti brewer who chooses to use hops has several options. The brewer in the Hellenius thesis boiled the hops in a small amount of water and then dumped the whole infusion into the wort. This method of introducing hops without a full wort boil is well-known among the raw-ale brewers of the Nordic and Baltic countries. Today this infusion is often referred to as *hop tea*, and some Lithuanian brewers even have a separate vessel for it, called the *hop tea cooker*. There are additional options: for example, some add hops to the mash or fermenter, whereas others infuse them in the wort as it exits the lauter tun.

Lautering

The most primitive beers were brewed by fermenting the mash—grain solids were in some way prevented from reaching the mouth. A lauter tun for filtering out the grain solids after mashing is an old innovation that today seems downright obvious.

Most farmhouse brewers in the Nordic and Baltic countries have a dedicated lauter tun. For each brew, the filter is formed from natural materials, such as straw and juniper twigs, holding the grain solids inside while the wort flows out through an opening below the filter. In most parts of Scandinavia and the Baltic countries, traditional brewers have used a wooden tub for lautering, while in Finland sahti brewers typically use

The largest hollowed-out-log kuurna I have ever seen is on display at the Linen and Sahti Museum in Lammi. The museum worker estimated that it can hold a mash from 310 pounds of grains (140 kilograms), yielding 80 gallons (300 liters) of sahti.

the kuurna, a trough-like lauter tun traditionally made from a hollowed-out log.

Thanks to its distinctive and charmingly primitive appearance, the kuurna has become symbolic of sahti. Yet similar farmhouse lauter tuns have been used elsewhere in northern Europe—for example, in the Baltic region (in Latvia) and in the Chuvash and Mari El republics of Russia. At first, the connection to Russia seems odd; after all, these two republics are about 900 miles (1,400 kilometers) away from the heartland of sahti. There's a Finno-Ugric connection perhaps (both Mari people and the Finns speak Finno-Ugric languages)?

A less exciting but more likely explanation is that in the northern woodlands a hollowed-out log is pretty much the simplest large vessel to make with primitive tools. Such containers were already used in the Stone

Age, before people figured out how to line up staves of wood to create a bucket. In Finland, similar vats have been used in preparing various foodstuffs, and for heating bath water with hot stones. In fact, kuurna-like vats might have been used as an early form of mash tun before skills in making large staved tubs grew.

Aspen has been a popular wood for kuurna use, because it is easy to hollow out. Pine has been used also, because it makes a very durable kuurna and large trunks are readily found. These vessels have been made for a wide variety of volumes, and with lengths ranging from less than 3 feet to over 10 feet (1 to 3 meters). Larger hollowed-out-log vats are suitable for producing at least 50 gallons (200 liters) of sahti.

To prepare the filter of a kuurna in the traditional way, wooden beams are aligned crosswise on the bottom, and then juniper twigs and long pieces of straw are laid lengthwise to rest on the beams. Rye or oat straw is typically favored. The juniper and lengths of straw are placed inside in layers, either juniper first and then straw or the other way around. The mash will be scooped on top of this filter. Some brewers also use layers of mash and straw alternately, especially when large amounts of rye malt or unmalted grain are used.

The beams leave space for flow at the bottom, and the trough is slightly inclined toward the end that has the bunghole. Usually all the mash is scooped into the kuurna before releasing the bung. When the bung is removed, the wort flowing out is at first very turbid, but it becomes gradually clearer as it flows through the filter formed by the grain bed. Most brewers pour the turbid first wort back on top of the mash and begin collecting the wort only when it runs clear.

Traditional hollowed-out-log kuurnas are still used in Finland, but today most kuurnas are made of stainless steel, with volumes ranging from less than 3 gallons to more than 500 gallons (10 to 2,000 liters). Kuurnas are also built of timber and plywood. Whatever the material, the shapes and usage have remained the same. Although with modern materials and heating systems it would be easy to build a single vessel incorporating the mash and lauter tuns, few traditional brewers have done so.

In modern kuurnas, the straw has been replaced with stainless steel wire mesh, but juniper branches are often laid on top of the mesh for flavor, even if unnecessary for filtering. Even some otherwise highly traditional setups include wire mesh instead of straw. Yet the tradition of

Modern kuurnas adhere to traditional shapes but vary widely in size. Commercial sahti brewery Lammin Sahti is equipped with "the world's biggest kuurna," holding 530 gallons (2,000 liters) of mash.

using straw is far from extinct, though the long pieces of straw need to be harvested by hand. Some brewers think that straw adds flavor to sahti.

The smoothness of the lautering depends not just on the filtering but also on the grinding level of the grain. Too fine a grind can make separation of liquid from solids difficult, while very coarse grinding can lead to poor extraction of malt sugars. In the old days, malt was ground with a hand-rotated stone mill, a *quern*, which was still used at some Finnish farmhouses in the early twentieth century.

Whereas in Finland farmhouse brewers use almost exclusively a kuurna for lautering, the traditional lauter tun used in Estonia, Sweden, and Norway is a wooden tub. Hollowed-out logs must have been utilized all over northern Europe, but a skilled cooper can likely build a large vessel from staves of wood in less time than it takes to find a huge tree, cut it down, and hollow it out. Besides, large trees are scarce in some prominent areas where traditional beers have thrived, such as the islands of the Baltic Sea. Tublike lauter tuns similar to Scandinavian and Estonian designs have been used in southwest and western Finland, but the tradition seems to have been lost.

A *kurnatõrs*, a traditional lautering tub from Saaremaa, Estonia. The filter is formed by bending wooden beams slightly above the bottom and then stacking juniper twigs and possibly straw on top of the twigs. Wort flow is controlled by lifting the tap at the bottom partially.

Regardless of the lauter tun's shape, the actual filter has been very similar between the Nordic and Baltic countries: juniper twigs and possibly straw resting on wooden props. Today most brewers have abandoned straw, relying on just a generous layer of juniper twigs.

While the wort is flowing from the lauter tun, it is customary to pour hot water or juniper infusion on top of the grain bed to rinse as much of the sugar from the grains as possible. Gradually adding water makes the flowing wort thinner, and the draining should be stopped before the wort as a whole gets too thin. Farmhouse brewers typically choose the stopping point by tasting the wort and judging its stickiness with a finger.

Because sahti should be strong, water must be used sparingly. Therefore, plenty of sugars remain in the grain. After the thick wort is collected for sahti, the grain bed can be rinsed further to make lower-alcohol beer from the "tails" of the wort. These days, farmhouse brewers seldom bother to collect these late runnings, but in olden times they were always utilized. I surveyed these late-runnings ales in the chapter "Low-Alcohol Farmhouse Ales" (page 96).

Fermentation

In the old days, fermentation was a magical event surrounded by various beliefs and rituals. For example, in the Nordic countries it was once customary to shout while adding the yeast—the louder the shouting, the stronger the ale would become. If the process went wrong, causes were often sought from the spiritual world. Perhaps somebody had offended the household spirit? Even today, a thunderstorm on a brew day might be blamed for fermentation problems affecting sahti.

After the wort has been drained from the lauter tun, and in some cases also boiled, it is cooled promptly, and the yeast is added. If cooling is delayed, beer-spoiling bacteria can take over the wort before the yeast does its work.

Cooling large volumes of liquid in wooden vessels is cumbersome, and in the old days this phase in brewing must have been nerve-rackingly slow. To speed up the cooling, the hot wort was, for example, divided across several buckets or drawn into a shallow, flat vat where evaporation aids in cooling. In any case, it was favorable to pitch yeast into very warm worts. According to ethnological surveys, yeast was added when the wort was no warmer than the hand or fresh milk. Some brewers tested the temperature by dipping their elbow into the wort, and at least with my elbow that corresponds to around 86°F (30°C).

By modern brewing standards, milk-warm temperature is exceptionally warm for brewer's yeast, and not even farmhouse brewers who use commercial baker's yeast dare to pitch at such high temperatures. The book *Yeast* by Chris White and Jamil Zainasheff states that "excessively high temperatures, 95°F (35°C) for ale yeast, will halt fermentation." Even if the yeast doesn't stop working, at high temperatures it can create an extravagant array of flavors.

The house yeasts might have adapted to such extreme temperatures. In Norway some brewers still pitch and ferment their traditional house strains at 104°F (40°C), which yields a solidly fruity flavor. Of commercial yeasts, the so-called saison strains are the best at withstanding temperatures above 86°F (30°C). It's hardly a coincidence that these yeasts were originally isolated from the farmhouse ales of Belgium.

On the other hand, there's an old Finnish saying that "the colder you ferment, the better the sahti you get." I suspect that this saying reflects the transition to commercial baker's yeasts and new types of dairy equipment in the twentieth century. Commercial baker's yeast was already being referred to in Finnish cookbooks in the early 1900s. At the same time, large aluminum containers for milk started to become common, and it is likely that these soon entered use for brewing as well, making cooling in a water bath easier.

Nowadays, the most popular fermentation temperature for sahti and koduõlu is in the range of 68–77°F (20–25°C), but there are notable exceptions. For example, in the village of Padasjoki, Finland, there is an at least decades-old tradition of fermenting sahti for several weeks at lager temperatures, around 50°F (10°C). Finnish fresh compressed baker's yeast seems to work this cold, but it is unknown whether other yeasts have been used in this manner.

Traditionally, the primary fermentation has been carried out in a wooden tub. An old trick is to clean the mash tun right after scooping the mash into the lauter tun, and use the mash tun as the fermenter. This is a very simple setup with only two large vessels: the combined mash tun and fermenting vessel and, second, the lauter tun. Some brewers in Finland and Estonia still employ this approach, although kettles and secondhand dairy tanks are now more typical instead of wooden tubs. Plastic tubs too are popular as fermenters. Often the fermenter is covered with a cloth, newspaper, or loosely fitted lid, but when touring farmhouse breweries, I have seen completely open fermenters also.

The primary fermentation of Nordic-Baltic farmhouse ales is typically short and vigorous, followed by a prompt transfer to cold storage. Determining the right moment for the transfer by tasting and inspecting the vigor of the foam is an essential part of the farmhouse brewer's skill. Timing depends a lot on the yeast and temperature, but today most sahtis and koduõlus are fermented warm for only one to three days.

Maturation and Storage

The farmhouse ale is often transferred into the cold while still fermenting a little, resulting in a slow secondary fermentation. This is an old preservation method: active yeast keeps spoilage bacteria at bay, and slowly released carbon dioxide prevents staling. Also, many sahti devotees prefer sweeter, slightly less fermented sahti.

Once cooled, most Nordic-Baltic farmhouse ales should be stored cold until serving. When the yeast stops working, the ale is more prone to spoilage. If souring bacteria are present, as is often the case with sahti, even a half day's storage at room temperature might give the bacteria a chance to ruin the beer.

Sahti casks at the Linen and Sahti Museum in Lammi.

Nordic-Baltic farmhouse ales are usually consumed very fresh, yet the beer will be better if some time is given for the yeast to settle and alcohol sharpness to smooth out. These days, sahti is usually served within two or three weeks from the brew day, but in olden times people didn't always wait that long. Prior to the 1970s, some sahtis were ready to serve within three or four days after brewing. Today in Lithuania, raw ales are typically served one week old. Norway has an old tradition of a tasting ceremony, *oppskåke*, in which the beer is moved from the fermenter to the cask about two days from brewing. Many heirloom farmhouse yeasts tend to drop out of solution very rapidly, allowing the ale to be served extremely fresh without a sensation of yeastiness.

In the transfer to colder conditions, the ale is usually scooped or racked into a fairly airtight container. Traditionally, this was a wooden cask, albeit somewhat different from the oak casks employed by commercial brewers or winemakers.

A Finnish farmhouse cask was usually made of pine and designed for either lying horizontally or standing vertically. Both designs had an opening on top for filling and cleaning. The opening was closed with a lid and sealed with dough made from rye flour. Ale was drawn out from a tap at the bottom above the dregs.

These casks were not easily transported long distances, and definitely they weren't made for rolling. Usually the ale was brewed in the house where the feasts were held. If the feast were to be elsewhere, the brewer rather than the ale came to that house.

Sahti casks were still used in the 1960s, and some brewers recall the hassles of cleaning and maintaining them. Considering that the beer was put in the cask early, leaving a thick layer of sediment in the cask, cleaning must have been an arduous task. No wonder these casks are mainly decorative items and museum artifacts today. There are exceptions, though. In Joutsa, Finland, the locals mentioned an old brewer who still kept his sahti in a wooden cask in the early 2010s.

Today sahti casks have been largely replaced with plastic canisters. These canisters are immensely practical though unaesthetic. They are easy to clean and easy to vent if the ale is still fermenting. They come in various sizes and cost little. Similar canisters are widely used to store farmhouse ales in other Nordic countries, and also farmhouse ciders in England are sometimes sold in them.

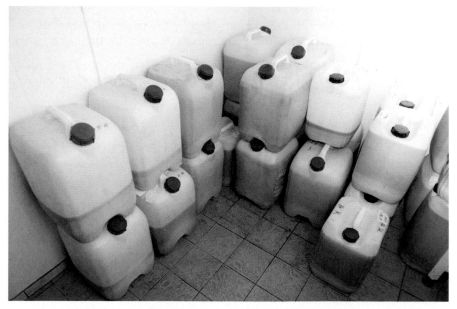

Plastic canisters are today's sahti casks—very handy and very ugly.

An ankur—a cask for storing, transporting, and serving koduõlu.

On the other hand, for someone new to the culture, a pour from a plastic canister can be really lackluster. Commercial brewery Lammin Sahti combated this image problem by selling the sahti in swing-top glass bottles and, more recently, in a stylish pouch. Glass bottles, however, require special attention since sahti can re-ferment and build up pressure.

In Estonia, koduõlu is stored in stainless steel casks specially fabricated by local craftsmen. A cask of this type goes by the name *ankur* (akin to "anchor" in English), just as the wooden casks do. This is already a several-decades-old tradition of its own. Paavo Pruul, a koduõlu master from Hiiumaa, reckoned that most ankurs still in use were made during the Soviet occupation, 1940–1991.

These charming steampunk-like cylindrical vessels come in various dimensions, from tall and slender to short and squat. Legs, handles, a threaded lid, and a tap have been welded onto them, and sometimes they have a pressure gauge also. An ankur will seal tightly, and it can be stored underwater. In Saaremaa, a man recalled diving into a well to retrieve his ankur after the attachment rope broke.

Maturation, transportation, and serving are done in these vessels. An ankur might be given to the brewer empty and collected full. Re-fermentation in the ankur can build up pressure, which sometimes results in a very lively koduõlu.

— III —
In Your Kitchen
or Brewery

Brewing sahti in a kitchen with kitchenware

— 12 —

Doing It Ourselves

Tips for Brewing

NOW IT IS TIME TO PUT THEORIES to the side and actually brew with prehistoric farmhouse techniques. Whether you are a home-brewer, craft brewer, or brewing virgin, I will now show you how to brew the ancient farmhouse ales in your brewery or kitchen. Even if traditional farmhouse ale is not your goal, these extraordinary techniques offer plenty of inspiration and tools for creating something new and unique. And if you've never brewed before, sahti might as well be your first brew, since these ales are far easier to brew and require less equipment than modern beer recipes do. I will offer tips on equipment, ingredients, and the brewing process here, while the actual recipes are saved for the last chapter (page 193) for convenient reference.

Brewing in line with folk tradition is an enlightening experience—and freeing. Many of the modern brewing rules can be broken, yet the beer still turns out to be excellent, and very different from today's beer. Traditional brewing isn't difficult, but it requires a mindset different from that in modern brewing:

- Nordic and Baltic farmhouse ales are very process-driven beers, and following the old techniques is the key to success. Proper ingredients alone won't yield authentic results.
- Some modern brewing practices have to be ignored. Modernizing the process on the basis of today's brewing knowledge leads in

Small batches of sahti can be easily brewed without dedicated brewing equipment. You can start with a household kettle and a colander.

many cases to more modern-tasting and less authentic farmhouse ale. Some techniques may seem like a recipe for disaster, but trust me: I have tested these things.

- Ignoring modern brewing practices and instruments does not mean sloppiness. In fact, the renowned masters are usually very consistent, and their success stems largely from meticulously applying practices that are known to work.
- Modern brewing equipment can be easily made to fit the old brewing processes. Wooden tubs and kuurnas would certainly look cool, but stainless steel doesn't rule out brewing the ancient way.
- You don't need exactly the same ingredients the Nordic farmhouse brewers use. Farmers have brewed with what is readily available, and so can you. These ales need not taste the same everywhere. This applies especially to juniper branches, which for many readers can be difficult to obtain.
- I'm afraid these ales cannot be brewed from malt extracts, in which malt has already been mashed, lautered, and processed into syrup or dry powder. To use a cooking analogy, you can't end up with a rare steak if somebody has already cooked it well-done.
- It is beautiful to see brewers getting inspired by the farmhouse techniques to create something new, but I have one request: reserve traditional names such as sahti, koduõlu, gotlandsdricke, maltøl, and kaimiškas for the brews that strive for authenticity.

Equipment

Most sahti brewers have two bigger brewing vessels: a tub for mashing and a kuurna for lautering. In contrast to modern brewing, you don't necessarily need a boil kettle, but most farmhouse brewers use a kettle or cauldron for heating water. In rough terms, 1 pound of grain makes 1 quart of sahti, and 1 pound of grain makes 1.5 to 2 quarts of mash. Therefore, the mashing and lautering vessels need to be about 1.5 to 2 times the batch volume.

Traditional wooden tubs and kuurnas are still used, but many brewers have adopted stainless steel versions of similar shape, because of the effort it takes to use and maintain wooden vessels. The choice of material

My combined mash–lauter tun, which I use for both sahti and modern-style beers. A slotted copper manifold takes the role of the filter, instead of juniper branches. The kettle is heated on a cooking plate. MIKA LAITINEN

doesn't have a huge flavor impact, but crafting, handling, and maintaining wooden gear are certainly honorable old-time skills.

A typical home or craft brewery setup with a combined mash and lauter tun works well for sahti-type ales. You will have no difficulties in replicating the process and getting the flavor right. In this setup, juniper branches are not laid in place for lautering; the juniper flavor can be extracted in other ways.

Sahti mashes are fairly thick, so mash tuns with external heating are the easiest to operate. Heating mash with water infusions will work too, but more attention is required for obtaining high enough temperatures and reasonable efficiency with a fairly small amount of water. The popular brew-in-a-bag (BIAB) method can be used, although in my opinion it is not ideal for thick mashes. In addition, BIAB can make for a very turbid sahti, because it lacks the wort-recirculation step for clarifying the wort.

Small batches of 1 or 2 gallons each can be made with standard kitchenware. A cooking pot can be used as a mash tun, and a big enough colander or strainer can serve as a kuurna. A simple "kuurna" can be easily made from a plastic bucket, a hose, and a length of copper pipe.

Most sahti brewers use a loosely covered open fermenter for the vigorous initial fermentation and a closed, tighter container after this for the secondary fermentation and storage. Typically, the initial fermenter is a plastic tub, metal milk churn, stainless steel kettle, or (in rare cases) wooden tub. Some brewers use the old farmhouse trick and put their mash tun to double duty as primary fermenter. Plastic canisters are the most typical vessels for secondary fermentation.

I have made many of the test brews for this book with a standard household kettle and this kind of "kuurna" made from a plastic bucket. It is a frugal option but works extremely well. The filter is made from a piece of copper pipe slotted with a hacksaw and pinched at the end. For this kind of tiny-scale brew system, small-diameter hose and pipe (e.g., ⅜-inch internal diameter) work the best. Choose a food-grade bucket and hose suitable for high temperatures. MIKA LAITINEN

Modern fermenters are convenient also for sahti, and two separate vessels are not always needed, as long as air contact and oxidation during secondary fermentation can be prevented. In any case, pressure buildup during maturation should be avoided by using an air lock or by releasing pressure occasionally.

The storage containers are usually chosen for easy checking and releasing of pressure. Farmhouse brewers typically use plastic canisters and PET bottles. Swing-top glass bottles are a good option too, if pressure buildup can be prevented with certainty. Alternatively, sahti can be kegged and pushed out with carbon dioxide, but if the traditional low carbonation is desired, release the keg pressure when storing sahti.

Malt and Unmalted Grain

The grain bill for sahti is usually very simple, often just one barley malt complemented with 5 to 10 percent dark rye malt. Today most Finnish sahti brewers use Viking's Sahti Malt for the barley and Kaljamallas for the dark rye. These malts are rarely seen outside Finland, but you don't need to sweat blood in efforts to source them. Considering how varied the traditional farmhouse malting practices once were, I see plenty of options.

In 2016 Colorado Malting Company started to distribute Viking's Sahti Malt in the United States, and a few European homebrew shops outside Finland sell this malt also. Hence, you might be able to get hold of the same malt Finns are using.

However, any combination of Pilsner, Vienna, and Munich malts will make a good sahti. My favorite barley malt bases use either Vienna malt alone or 20 percent Munich malt with 80 percent Pilsner or Vienna malt. These options are not aimed at replicating Viking's Sahti Malt, but they do fit the taste profile nicely.

Kaljamallas is a unique Finnish lightly roasted rye malt (color unit is around 180 EBC, or 70°L). This malt is made by Laihian Mallas and, as far as I know, is not exported. Although it is not a caramel malt, I recommend replacing it with caramel rye malt, which lends a rich dark rye bread character appropriate for sahti. Caramel rye malt is now produced by several North American and European malt houses. Usually these have a color close to that of Kaljamallas. Much darker chocolate rye malt

(500–800 EBC, or 200–300°L) is available too, but such malt should be used with caution, and only in small amounts for color. Dark roasted malt can give an inappropriate sharp edge to sahti.

Fans of rye might choose to replace some of the barley malt with pale rye malt or unmalted rye. Ten percent pale rye malt in addition to dark rye malt is a conservative starting point, and from 20 percent onward the flavor gets more assertive. Using 5 to 10 percent unmalted rye, oats, and/or wheat can be a good way to hone the recipe, adding a nice rustic, grainy edge and smooth mouthfeel. Traditional sahti brewers use unmalted grains in the form of flour or coarse grits, but flakes will work too.

Today smoked malt is rarely used in sahti, but in light of the history of home malting in a smoke sauna or riihi, it is a valid addition and suited well to the flavor profile. Alder-smoked malt would be typical for the Nordic countries, but German beech-smoked malt is not a bad option either. If you take this route, I recommend shooting for smooth but noticeable smokiness.

Yeast

Authentic sahti calls for baker's yeast or a traditionally maintained farmhouse yeast culture. Of course, if strict authenticity is not your goal, you may brew farmhouse wort and ferment it as you please. In any case, I have some interesting options for you.

Suomen Hiiva's fresh compressed baker's yeast is by far the most popular sahti yeast, but it is difficult to obtain outside Finland. All is not lost, though. Nordic and Baltic farmhouse brewers have used various European brands of baker's yeast with good results. I have tested several fresh and dried baker's yeasts, and every one of them has made decent sahti. Therefore, I suggest brewing your first sahti with a local baker's yeast.

Each brand of baker's yeast probably is its own strain so will ferment in its own way. Baker's yeasts seem to produce fruity flavors in general, but of the brands I have tested only Suomen Hiiva has produced assertive banana and clove flavors.

The amount of yeast pitched varies hugely from brewer to brewer, but ⅔ ounce fresh baker's yeast for 5 gallons of wort (20 grams for 20 liters) is a fairly typical pitch. With dry baker's yeast, a third of that amount is enough. Before pitching, fresh baker's yeast can be liquefied in a small amount of cool water, but dry baker's yeast will be liveliest if rehydrated in the way dried brewer's yeast is:

> Add dry yeast to a small amount of 95 to 104°F (35 to 40°C) water. Stir gently to break up clumps, and let rest for fifteen minutes. Stir again, and wait ten minutes. Then add a small amount of cooled wort to the mix, wait another ten minutes, and pitch the yeast into the wort. The last step is not absolutely necessary, but it helps the yeast adapt to its new conditions in the wort, the fermentation temperature in particular.

Norwegian farmhouse yeast (kveik) is an extremely interesting alternative to baker's yeast. To my mind, true farmhouse kveiks without laboratory treatment would comply with the TSG appellation of sahti—a traditionally maintained kveik would count as "harvested yeast" in the appellation, since sahti brewers had similar house yeasts in the past. In contrast, a commercial lab-purified kveik is hardly a traditional sahti yeast. That said, it will make a great sahti-like ale.

Even a laboratory-treated single-strain kveik captures a great deal of unique brewing history, and these yeasts are now internationally available to both home and craft brewers through several yeast laboratories, such as Omega Yeast Labs, the Yeast Bay, Escarpment Laboratories, Mainiacal Yeast Labs, and the National Collection of Yeast Cultures. Some of these yeasts are sold in select homebrew shops all over the world.

Some sahti recipes in the literature suggest adding lactic bacteria to mimic rustic farmhouse fermentation. That would be considered foolishness by any traditional brewer, and I see no point in intentionally infecting the ale. After all, farmhouse brewers have been trying hard to avoid sourness. Nevertheless, unboiled farmhouse wort will make a tasty—even if untraditional—sour ale.

Juniper

In traditional sahti districts juniper is an uncomplicated ingredient. The only available species is *Juniperus communis* of subspecies *communis*, and it is found almost everywhere in nature. Brewers typically collect the branches from trees in their backyard or a nearby forest without even measuring the amounts used. In other parts of the world, obtaining juniper branches might be more complicated, but that shouldn't keep you from brewing sahti.

Though juniper is ubiquitous, the juniper trees in North America, for example, might look completely different from Finnish juniper and provide a distinctly different taste. To my mind, we can welcome this diversity and brew sahti with various kinds of branches, as long as the ingredient is edible and tastes good. I see no need to stick to the species *J. communis*, but bear in mind that some juniper species may be toxic. Also, steer clear of branches sold for decorative purposes, since they may contain preservatives.

If we accept various kinds of junipers for inclusion in the ingredient list, we might as well think about the original purpose of the branches as a filtering and cleaning aid. Why not turn to other trees in this manner as well, and use branches of birch, spruce, or something else? This approach is more in the "inspired by" category, but the results can be extraordinary.

Before you brew with your local twigs of juniper, or any other tree, you should judge the flavor. Some brewers have commented that North American juniper doesn't always taste pleasant, describing the flavor as very woody, piney, and earthy. Make an infusion from the twigs with the technique described below and taste it. If you find the flavor pleasing, you will like that flavor in a beer as well. If not, it can't hurt to consider other options.

Berries don't exactly replicate branches, but they are an acceptable substitute. I like the flavor of juniper berries, and they do capture the scent of a Nordic forest well. Half an ounce of berries for 5 gallons (15 grams for 20 liters), added to the hot wort during lautering, is a good starting point.

Most sahti folks prefer a delicate juniper flavor, and most of them would also agree that none is always better than too much. An overload of branches, especially when used as an infusion, can create a stinging and solventy sharpness, which is going to stand out unpleasantly. Remember also that sahti need not contain any juniper whatsoever. Well-made sahti should taste excellent even without juniper.

Brewers using a traditional kuurna may lay the branches on the bottom of the kuurna. This kind of juniper filter extracts some flavor from the branches, but usually the flavor will not be excessive, even with a fairly large number of branches.

Another use of juniper branches is for the infusion. There are as many ways of making juniper infusion as there are brewers. Some boil branches in water for two hours, while others simmer without boiling. Some infuse for an hour, others overnight. This is my preferred method:

> Bring the water to a boil, and turn off the heat. Add branches such that they float loosely, and let infuse for at least an hour. The infusion should look reddish brown, much like a bright wort. Note that juniper resins will coat the vessel in which you are making this infusion, and you may need some elbow grease to clean it.

This infusion can be used for cleaning, mashing, and sparging. For when you're using the infusion as flavoring for the first time, I suggest making your brew water from one part infusion to two parts plain water. Taste the infusion, and you will gradually learn the connection between the flavor of your infusion and the results in the ale. Then you can start to adjust the quantity of branches and the infusion to your taste.

Admittedly, I'm often lazy and just throw juniper branches into the mash. This is not a traditional method, but it produces an authentic flavor and works well with modern brewing setups. Perhaps for pH reasons, a surprisingly small quantity is needed: for a 5-gallon batch, adding ⅓ ounce of branches (10 grams for 20 liters) into the mash is a good starting point.

Hops

I see no need to use hops in sahti, but subtle hop character is not against the tradition. Authentic contemporary sahti has no hop flavor or bitterness to speak of. Elsewhere in the Nordic and Baltic region, small hop additions are fairly typical, and hops are pretty much required in the Lithuanian kaimiškas tradition.

If you're hopping your ale, I recommend whole hops with a low bitterness content. Homegrown hops would be ideal, but many farmhouse brewers use commercial hops.

Farmhouse brewers have used hops in various ways, but I have found the hop tea method the most useful, since it gets the most out of the hops without a need to boil the wort. It adds both bitterness and flavor, though not as much as the conventional wort boil. This is my standard hop tea method:

> Boil whole hop cones in a small amount of water for one hour. Use just enough water to cover the hops, around 2 quarts for 3 ounces of hops (2 liters for 100 grams). When lautering, sieve the hoppy liquid into the wort and place the used hops on the lauter tun's grain bed, so that they get rinsed while you are sparging the mash.

If you want to brew as the Lithuanian farmhouse brewers do, make this kind of hop tea by using 2 or 3 ounces of hops per 5-gallon batch (60 to 90 grams for 20 liters).

Cleanliness

Although farmhouse ales are often brewed in fairly bacteria-rich environments, not even the most traditional brewers can afford to overlook cleaning. In particular, debris in the vessels or containers touching cold wort or ale can be a source of nasty-tasting infections.

Equipment at a modern brewery is cleaned of visible dirt and then sanitized. In essence, traditional farmhouse brewers do the same thing: cleaning is done with water and elbow grease. After this, wooden vessels and utensils are soaked or rinsed with hot juniper water. In essence, juniper water is used like a sanitizer, and for wood this remains an excellent approach.

For modern materials I recommend modern cleaning agents and sanitizers available in homebrew shops. Plastic tubing and containers that cannot be sanitized by heat benefit especially from today's cleaning chemicals.

Making the Wort

Today's brewers have various kinds of equipment and objectives, so I will now address several options for mashing, lautering, and boiling. I'll give all the numbers that modern brewers want to see, but if you prefer to brew in a more historically authentic way, you may as well ignore the numeric details and follow the principles without exact measurements.

Most sahti brewers mash for four to nine hours, raising the temperature slowly from hand-warm to very hot. This age-old technique works well without a thermometer and with rustic homemade malt. If I were giving a historical brewing demonstration, I would probably mash this way, with the wetting technique described on page 146. However, I have noticed that a far simpler procedure gets the most out of today's commercial malt. That said, I hope that nobody defiles a traditional family recipe on the basis of my advice.

After testing various mashing times and temperatures, I have finally settled on a procedure described in my recipe for homebrewer's sahti (see page 202). The technique is similar to the traditional sahti mash, but I have omitted the lower-temperature steps and shortened the rests. In my home brewery, this 140/158/176°F (60/70/80°C) approach takes about two and a half hours, and it can be reverted to the traditional process if steps at 104°F (40°C) and 122°F (50°C) are added and the rest periods are lengthened. With a high proportion of rye malt or unmalted grains,

Sahti master Hannu Sirén cleans his mashing vat right after the mash has been scooped out.

the lower-temperature rests are useful, because they break down highly viscous beta glucans that are present especially in rye and oats.

A single-infusion mash will also work, especially if the proportion of rye and unmalted grain is kept below 15 percent. The efficiency may be lower, but extending the mashing time to two or three hours may help. Nordic and Baltic farmhouse brewers using a single infusion tend to opt for fairly high temperatures in the range of 154–162°C (68–72°C).

Sahti brewers often favor high final mash temperatures, and some even bring the whole mash to a boil before lautering. If you can, I recommend raising the mash to above 167°F (75°C), since this boosts the extraction of malt sugars. With a water-infusion-heated mash tun, consider performing a decoction: place a portion of the mash in a kettle, boil it, and return it to the main mash. Adventurous brewers can experiment with a full mash boil.

Both efficient utilization of malt and sparing use of water are important in making high-gravity sahti. Because sahti wort is not concentrated by boiling, relatively little water must be used to rinse the mash during lautering. Overly diluted wort is among typical beginner's mistakes. Whatever mashing practices you use, the mash should be fairly thick, using no more than 1.2 quarts of water for 1 pound of grain (2.5 liters/kilogram). Less water in the mash leaves more water for sparging, which helps in extracting the malt sugars. My own preference is for a mash thickness of 1.1 quarts per pound (2.3 liters/kilogram). This is nicely stirrable, while still leaving water for rinsing.

At the beginning of lautering, most sahti brewers recirculate the wort back over the mash until the wort runs clear. With raw ales lacking a wort boil, this step really makes a difference, and without it all kinds of turbid substances (lipids, polyphenols, and proteins) would get carried over into the final ale.

In the final stages of lautering, the mash is sparged with hot water. According to brewing science, the water should be no warmer than 172°F (78°C), to prevent the risk of tannins being leached from the malt husks. Traditional brewers sparge with hot or boiling water without measuring the temperature, and I see no problem in that. In sweet sahti a small amount of tannins can even be a desirable balancing factor, and the amount of sparge water will be fairly small in any event. When lautering comes to an end, beware diluting the wort too much—you cannot boil

Whether modern or traditional, brewers are always bending the "rules." This sahti master puts juniper branches *on top of* the mash in the kuurna, and he then rinses the branches with hot wort. He claims that he obtains smoother and gentler juniper flavoring this way. MIKA LAITINEN

down the volume later. Traditional brewers often decide on the cutoff point with various rules of thumb, but stopping at a predetermined volume is the easiest rule to apply.

When all the wort has been collected, the final question is "to boil or not to boil?" I recommend leaving the wort unboiled. That will give you a more traditional ale that stands out from any craft beer. I know from personal experience that brewers who have read their textbooks would like to add a short boil as a sanitary precaution, but that really isn't necessary, as I have argued throughout this book. If you must boil, keep it to no more than ten minutes, which will still leave plenty of the proteins typical of sahti.

For cooling the wort there are no special farmhouse tricks. Most brewers cool in a water bath, and you can use whatever method is at your disposal. After cooling, modern brewers tend to filter out the sediment known as *trub*, but without a boil or with only a short boil that isn't required; just dump all the wort into the fermenter.

Modern brewers typically aerate their wort before fermentation, but traditional brewers rarely do this, apart from inadvertent splashing. I see no need for an aeration stage, but if your ale finishes sweeter than you would like, consider adding a short aeration step next time.

Fermentation

Let's first recap original farmhouse fermentation: Pitch the yeast as soon as the wort has cooled to hand-warm temperature, ferment in a tub for a short time, move the ale to a cask, and condition briefly in the cold. Store cool until serving.

This brewing folk tradition has been optimized for wooden vessels, less effective cooling methods, and mixed house yeast cultures that may contain souring bacteria. Commercial baker's yeast brought some changes to this tradition, but the fermentation of sahti is still out of the ordinary:

- Most sahti brewers ferment for twelve to forty-eight hours at 64 to 77°F (18 to 25°C) and then chill the ale as soon as the fermentation begins to calm down. At this stage, the yeast's work may not be completely finished, and slow secondary fermentation might continue in the cold. With this option, timing and obtaining the desired level of sweetness are challenging.
- Some brewers let their sahti finish fermenting fully in warm conditions but transfer the ale to the cold immediately afterward. Often they do the fermentation at slightly lower temperatures, 63 to 68°F (17 to 20°C), a level at which baker's yeast is less expressive and easier to control. Waiting until fermentation has finished has its benefits, but if cooling doesn't begin promptly enough, souring bacteria could spoil the ale. Arguably, this option is a slightly greater deviation from the original tradition.
- A few brewers ferment sahti slowly in a cellar for several weeks until the time of serving. Often yeast is added at room temperature, after which the sahti is moved to a cellar below 59°F (15°C) at the first signs of fermentation. With this approach, a lot of expertise is required to guarantee proper fermentation

and having the ale ready at the right moment. This lager-style fermentation works with Finnish fresh compressed yeast, but I suspect that most baker's yeast would come to a halt at such a low temperature.

Modern books on brewing often advise keeping the ale in warm conditions for a few days after fermentation seems to have ceased, but with farmhouse fermentation this isn't always a good idea. If the yeast contains souring bacteria, as baker's yeast and some traditional kveiks do, the bacteria may become active as soon as the yeast starts slowing down. Therefore, cooling the ale before the yeast is completely done is an effective way to prevent souring.

I cannot stress the importance of this technique enough. This trick enables you to achieve nonsour fermentation even if the yeast culture has its share of alien bacteria. On the other hand, if you cool your ale too early, the brew will end up cloyingly sweet, and it might re-ferment unpredictably later on. The timing of the warm-to-cold transfer is a critical skill of a farmhouse brewer, which is learned gradually by doing.

Finnish baker's yeast often ferments explosively above 68°F (20°C), which makes the timing even trickier—this monster of a yeast might produce 7 percent ABV in less than a day and then halt before you know it. We're fortunate that some other baker's yeasts prove easier to handle, and with them I recommend fermenting at ambient temperatures of 64 to 80°F (18 to 27°C). Anything warmer than that creates a risk of the baker's yeast getting too expressive and uncontrollable. With baker's yeast, your ale is likely to be fermented within a day or two, but sometimes you have to wait for three or four days to pass. In any case, it is best to monitor the progress, taste often, and be prepared to move the ale into the cold soon. While your ale is stored in the cold, check regularly to make sure the vessel isn't building up pressure.

If you get hold of kveik, I recommend fermenting as its original owner does, probably at 86 to 104°F (30 to 40°C). Commercial kveiks may work more slowly than the original farmhouse version, but I would still be surprised if a kveik fermentation at these typical warm temperatures takes more than five days. Commercial kveik has been cleaned of bacteria, and that makes things much easier. Your ale will not go sour if you wait a little longer to make sure fermentation has finished. That way, you don't need to worry about the ale going sour or re-fermenting later on. You may even store and transport the ale in warm conditions for a few days.

The cold conditioning of sahti is typically short, and the ale should be ready to drink as soon as the majority of the yeast has settled. During conditioning, rough edges such as alcohol sharpness will smooth out, and well-made sahti should be in top condition within one to three weeks from brew day.

Traditional brewers usually scoop or rack sahti from the fermenter to storage containers just before cold conditioning. With baker's yeast, which usually doesn't settle easily, this practice creates lots of yeast sediment in the storage containers. Hence, another racking might be needed if the sahti has to be transported. If you have a fermenter equipped with an air lock, you might as well delay the racking until most yeast has settled, so that one racking should be enough. Most kveiks clump together extremely swiftly, enabling one to serve the ale very fresh, sometimes even at less than a week old.

One master keeps his sahti in plastic canisters cooled by a spring in the forested countryside of Finland. To make storage easier, he has built a shed around the spring. Despite the highly rural location, someone once stole his sahti. So now the shed has a lock on the door and security bars on the windows. MIKA LAITINEN

In Finland sahti is served without any added carbonation whatsoever, but, as I explained in the chapter "Drinking Sahti," soft carbonation from residual fermentation is well within the bounds of the tradition. Getting this fizz from residual fermentation can be difficult and unpredictable, however.

People new to this kind of traditional ale sometimes have difficulty enjoying completely still beer. Before you learn to appreciate uncarbonated beer, or the necessary tricks of residual fermentation, I don't mind if you cheat a little bit. If kegging, you may add a small shot of carbon dioxide. Priming your ale with a dose of sugar is problematic, because re-fermentation at warm temperatures would expose the ale to bacteria. With a commercial kveik, in contrast, this priming will work fine.

By now I should have you convinced that cold storage is essential for avoiding sourness whenever your yeast contains souring bacteria. Even if the ale is not in danger of going sour, lower temperatures will slow down the staling of raw ale. Depending on temperature, even sahti in cold storage may still go sour at some point: at first, the taste becomes drier, after which some tartness appears, before the taste finally becomes noticeably acidic. It is a matter of personal preference when the sourness has grown unpleasant. If your sahti shows signs of souring and you happen to like sour ales, please consider storing some for a year or two—you might have an "ugly duckling."

— 13 —

Re-creating Medieval and Viking Ales

Brew Like a Viking

BREWING SAHTI IS RE-CREATING MEDIEVAL ALE, but if you are into a
more specific era or part of Europe, the tips here will take you further.
When it comes to medieval and Viking Age ale, the following elements
of beer culture are perhaps the most interesting:

- **Gruit ale** is the best known medieval ale. It was popular in the
  early Middle Ages and High Middle Ages. Somewhat confusingly, today *gruit ale* may refer to any beer without hops, but I
  restrict my use of the term to the historical ales that included
  gruit, a mysterious herbal mixture that was highly controlled and
  taxed by the authorities.
- **Ales of medieval England** should not be ignored when one
  is talking about medieval brewing. In England archaic-style
  unhopped ales were made throughout the medieval era, and in
  some locations even after that. For this reason, the best written
  accounts come from England.
- **Viking ales** are difficult to pin down, but plenty of indirect information can be used to extract information about the ales of this
  intriguing era.
- **Hopped beer** in the late Middle Ages paved the way for modern
  beer. This is a fascinating era in the history of beer, but now I will
  concentrate on the more exotic unhopped ales.

What the hell is he doing? He is re-creating Viking ale. COURTESY OF SAMI BRODKIN

These are very broad categories that feature plenty of diversity. Cities, castles, estates, monasteries, and farmhouses probably all had different cultures of brewing. For instance, the poor drank weaker ale than well-to-do people. From very early on there were beer styles, even within one particular region and era. So I can provide only a peek into an extremely broad topic.

The historical background on these ales was presented in the chapter "History of Farmhouse Ales," so now I will concentrate mostly on practical brewing tips. It seems sensible to conclude that the brewing process for these unhopped ales lacked a wort boil and employed techniques similar to those for sahti. Therefore, the advice in the previous chapter, "Doing It Ourselves," will apply here as well, and the main additional knowledge you need involves a few more facts about medieval ingredients. A recipe template for gruit ale, medieval English ale, and Viking ale waits for you in the next chapter, "Recipes."

Medieval Brewing Herbs

Hunting for herbs for beer and food is another hobby of mine, which allows me to share with you my experience of how to obtain, process, and use some of the essential medieval brewing herbs. I have tested all these herbs in my home brewery.

Bog myrtle (*Myrica gale*) is surrounded by incredible confusion related to safety concerns. It is described as poisonous in several books and plant databases, and some databases state that it should not be eaten by pregnant woman, because it can induce abortion. It is widely believed that it adds to the potency of ale and that larger quantities of it in ale cause headaches and a terrible hangover. Stories of the Vikings driving themselves berserk with bog myrtle before battle are often repeated in the literature. How on earth did such a plant become one of the most popular medieval beer spices?

There is more to the story: bog myrtle has been declared nonpoisonous by the USDA and the Finnish Poison Information Centre. Some commercial beers and fine-dining dishes are seasoned with this herb. I have brewed several ales with it and not noticed any side effects—no headache, hangover, or berserk rage, though I can readily accept that bog myrtle is a stimulant.

Surely this is a matter of dosage, as with many medicinal or culinary plants: small amounts are safe, but side effects or even toxicity may arise with larger quantities. While I have brewed with all the herbs introduced here and tested the recommended amounts, I advise you to exercise your judgment before using bog myrtle, or yarrow, ground ivy, sage, and rosemary, described below. Some of the stories about unpleasant side effects may well be true but a result of large doses of these herbs.

However, I'm pretty sure that the Vikings going berserk from bog myrtle before a battle is a myth, based solely on speculation. The Vikings likely seasoned their ales with bog myrtle, and I can also believe that extreme quantities of this herb can lead to a frenzy. Yet nobody seems able to provide evidence of any kind that the berserkers actually went berserk by drinking or eating something. Furthermore, many historians and archaeologists take the stories of the berserkers as legends that make separating fact from fiction impossible.

The desired flavors of bog myrtle are mainly in the leaves, and the stems contribute mostly woodiness. The scent is powerful, with a potent perfume of plenty of camphor and pine. Bog myrtle leaves contain tannic bitterness that is somewhat different from that of hops. As with hops, the

Dried bog myrtle in the mash. This was a successful test brew in research for the book, and the recipe can be found on page 209. MIKA LAITINEN

longer you steep them in hot mash, wort, or water, the more tannins and bitterness you get.

Bog myrtle is usually dried in the form of sprigs. I know a farmhouse brewer who makes an infusion from whole sprigs, but usually herb gatherers chop off the woodier parts of the stems after drying. The woodier parts wouldn't taint the brew, but since they are bulky and merely add woody tannins, it is best to get rid of most of them. Bog myrtle grows in both Europe and North America, but only in certain wetlands. For many it is difficult to collect, but a few online shops sell dried leaves of it.

Wild rosemary (*Rhododendron tomentosum* or *Ledum palustre*) is fairly often mentioned as a brewing herb for both gruit ales and Nordic farmhouse ales. Likely it was a poor man's substitute for bog myrtle. It is generally considered poisonous, and I advise avoiding it. Some people even get a headache from walking in a swamp where it grows.

Many sources claim that **yarrow** (*Achillea millefolium*) was a typical constituent of gruit, but that is perhaps a misconception. I think the claim is rooted in another misconception, that the gruit region extended to the Nordic area. Medieval Nordic brewers did brew herb ales with both yarrow and bog myrtle, but there wasn't a monopoly on these herbs. Nor do Nordic sources support the common conception that bog myrtle and yarrow were mixed together. It seems that in the Nordic region bog myrtle or yarrow were optional brewing herbs, and only one of the two was used for any single brew.

Yarrow has many of the qualities of bog myrtle, and it is an obvious candidate for gruit. Yet there's not much evidence that it actually was used in true gruit. Perhaps the best survey on what herbs ended up in gruit has been provided by historian Roel Mulder, who collected data from older articles based on the archives of several German and Dutch towns in the fourteenth and fifteenth centuries. The data clearly show that bog myrtle was the primary gruit herb and that wild rosemary was used whenever bog myrtle wasn't. Then, somewhat oddly, there were fairly rare secondary spices of laurel berry and laserwort. Yarrow is completely absent from these records.

Anyway, yarrow is an interesting medieval brewing herb. In moderate quantities, it is generally considered safe for consumption, but it is also believed to increase the effects of alcohol. I have used it several times, without ever experiencing any side effects. The taste of yarrow is highly

Dried yarrow, ready to be thrown into a brew. The whole plant is useful for flavoring. MIKA LAITINEN

complex and peculiar, with bitter-tonic qualities and flavors of Christmas spices and cloudberry in the flowers.

Yarrow is a stubborn weed in many parts of the world and fairly easy to harvest. The whole plant is useful in brewing: the leaves, flowers, and stems each have a flavor of their own. I have noticed that the flowers taste good only in the early stages of blossoming and soon turn dull and soapy. The stalks contain more bitter tannins, and you may reduce that effect by collecting more of the leafy and flowery tops.

Ground ivy (*Glechoma hederacea*) is another fine old-time brewing herb. It has been especially popular among English brewers, and its use probably goes back to Anglo-Saxon times. The earthy and aromatic flavor is reminiscent of thyme. The leaves add tannins also, and the astringent qualities increase toward the end of summer. The leaves are the main flavor-givers, but flowers and stems can be thrown into the brew as well.

Sage (*Salvia officinalis*) and **rosemary** (*Rosmarinus officinalis*) are popular culinary herbs, but they also have a venerable history as beer flavorings. These herbs might have been part of some gruits, but again there is little evidence of that. These are powerfully aromatic herbs with camphor, herbal bitterness, and astringent tannins. Sage produces more menthol notes and bitterness, while rosemary adds a piney touch. You may use only the leaves or instead whole sprigs. If you feel uncomfortable using bog myrtle or have difficulties in obtaining it, you can use either of these herbs just as well, or a blend of the two. Flavor-wise, these are excellent substitutes for bog myrtle.

In the past, brewing herbs were often dried, but you might as well use them fresh if you can. I often freeze fresh brewing herbs for later use, and it works like a charm. In weighing the herbs, you need to take into account that fresh plants weigh a lot more than dried. With most herbs the rule used with hops seems to apply: use four to five times more of the fresh than the dried herb. Bog myrtle seems to be more dryish, and with it I recommend using only two to three times more of the fresh.

We have only vague ideas as to when in the process medieval brewers added their herbs. It is commonly thought that gruit herbs were mixed with the malt, so that the herbs ended up in the mash. Making an herb infusion and using that as brew water would yield a similar effect. Adding the herbs to the hot wort while collecting it is another option. At least sometimes, herbs were added to the fermenting or finished ale.

I recommend adding half of the herbs to the mash and the other half to the wort. The mash addition will give more tannins, woodiness, and bitterness that was likely typical for medieval herbal ales. The wort addition will contribute more aroma and flavor. When making a raw ale, add herbs to the wort while lautering. If you decide to boil your wort, steep the latter portion in the hot wort after shutting off the heat and before cooling, for ten minutes or so. If after the most vigorous fermentation your ale seems to be lacking in herbs, you can always put more herbs into the fermenter.

Ground ivy grows wild in many parts of the world, and some deem it an invasive weed. I consider myself lucky because it thrives naturally in my garden. MIKA LAITINEN

We have only distant clues to indicate how strongly flavored the medieval ales were. I believe the flavor of these herbs was noticeable but not excessive. The table below shows quantities that have worked well in my homebrewed farmhouse ales. The suggested quantities are substantial, but in sweet and robust farmhouse ales the flavor will not be overpowering.

These same herbs will nicely spice up contemporary brews as well, but for modern ales with a standard wort boil I recommend slightly different approach: halve the quantities shown in the table below, and add herbs only to the hot wort, steeping ten to twenty minutes before cooling.

Suggested quantities of medieval and Viking Age brewing herbs, in ounces per 5 gallons, or grams per 20 liters. The amounts are for single-herb brews. If mixing herbs, reduce the amount correspondingly. For example, try a blend of .25 ounces fresh rosemary and .33 ounces fresh sage.

Herb	Amount fresh	Amount dried
Bog myrtle	1.33 ounces (40 grams)	0.67 ounces (20 grams)
Yarrow	2.67 ounces (80 grams)	0.67 ounces (20 grams)
Ground ivy	2.67 ounces (80 grams)	0.67 ounces (20 grams)
Sage	0.67 ounces (20 grams)	0.17 ounces (5 grams)
Rosemary	0.5 ounces (15 grams)	0.17 ounces (5 grams)

In the selection of herbs for medieval and Viking ales, these are the key points, in my view:

- Bog myrtle was the primary herb in gruit, and I believe this herb on its own will capture the essence of gruit. Sage and rosemary may not be typical gruit herbs, but in terms of flavor they are excellent substitutes for bog myrtle, especially in a half-and-half blend.
- In his work as a beer historian, Martyn Cornell has uncovered a great deal of evidence suggesting that medieval English ales were often brewed without any herbs or hops. Brew a raw ale from only malt, water, and yeast, and you will notice that it doesn't lack balance or flavor.

- Nevertheless, various herbs did end up in medieval English ales, but perhaps including only a single herb at a time would be most historically accurate. Ground ivy, rosemary, and sage would be typical herbs, though there are many others.
- Juniper, bog myrtle, and yarrow were part of some mixed fermented drinks before the Viking Age. They have been used by Nordic farmhouse brewers for the last few centuries as well. Therefore, these three plants are the most probable flavorings for Viking ales.

Medieval Grain Bills

Old heirloom varieties of grain malted in traditional farmhouse style would be a good approximation of medieval malt, but since very few of us have access to that kind of malt, I will now discuss how to mimic the grains of yore with modern malt.

In the past, malt provided less sugar than today, and old-time brewers had to compensate for that by using large amounts of malt. However, more malt inevitably means more brew water, and hence more diluted wort. This limited the gravity and strength of medieval brews.

My educated guess is that historical malt yielded only two thirds the extract when compared to modern malt. In practice this assumption means that if a farmhouse brewer obtains a gravity of 27°P from modern malt, which is quite an achievement, historical malt would give that brewer only 18°P. By this reasoning, I presume that medieval ales rarely exceeded a gravity of 18°P, or alcohol content of around 7 percent, at least without honey. My medieval ale recipe is written with these limitations in mind.

Medieval malt was usually smoky from kilning with open fire, but the flavor and amount of smoke varied a lot, depending on the fuel and kiln type. You can mimic the taste with commercial smoked malt or smoke some malt yourself. Using smoked malt for 10 to 20 percent of the grain is a conservative starting point for gruit ales or medieval English ales. On the basis of traditional malting techniques of Norway and Gotland, I'm inclined to think that the Viking ales were very, very smoky. I mean smokier than an ale brewed solely from commercial beech-smoked malt. In my Viking ale recipe, half of the malt is smoked, and that is likely to be an understatement.

Still, I think it is better to go easy at first on the smoky flavor. Today people are less accustomed to flavors of smoke, and you don't need to

The Vikings must have adapted their brewing to the local conditions when they landed. There is no single Viking way to brew. I'm pretty sure, though, that while the Vikings were in the Nordic climes they brewed with juniper.
COURTESY OF SAMI BRODKIN

torment yourself or your guests with liquid bonfire purely for the sake of historical accuracy.

Many medieval English and Dutch recipes featured large quantities of oats. Oats were usually a lot cheaper than barley, but it is difficult to determine whether that was the main reason for using them. In any case, using oat malt or unmalted oats (flakes are the easiest to brew with) as part of the grain bill is worth some experimenting.

Medieval Fermentation

I truly believe that an heirloom yeast from a Nordic or Baltic farmer would be the best approximation to medieval fermentation. We don't know for sure that medieval brewers had this kind of yeast, but, seriously, what could be a better option?

A yeast that hasn't been purified in a laboratory would be the most authentic, but using and maintaining such a yeast with traditional methods would require lots of practice and patience. I recommend starting with a commercial kveik or brewer's yeast, learning the basics of how to brew raw ales before having to worry about tricky fermentation. That would already be more authentic than most "medieval" ales sold today.

Obviously, commercial baker's yeast isn't an authentic medieval ingredient, but it would teach you how to deal with souring bacteria. A final, hardcore option would be to learn the traditional yeast-handling techniques that farmhouse brewers have been using for centuries. If you want to go in this direction, I'm sure somebody can provide a farmhouse culture to get you started.

– 14 –

Recipes

Examples and Starting Points

THE NINE RECIPES IN THIS CHAPTER offer examples of traditional farmhouse ales and a starting point for your own brews. Even if you are not about to brew, I recommend reading the first four recipes, from true farmhouse masters. They will give you a good idea of how sahti and koduõlu are brewed today.

The other five recipes are my own design and aimed at folks stepping into the world of Nordic farmhouse brewing. Three of these recipes are in the vein of sahti tradition but from the perspective of a modern brewer or a newbie. The final two recipes use the tradition as a stepping-stone to crafting a new beer or re-creating medieval ale.

Recipe Specifics

I have tried to keep the farmhouse masters' recipes as close as possible to the originals while still providing enough information for replicating them. This wasn't an easy task, since normally the farmhouse "recipe" isn't written down—it is learned by word of mouth and by watching and assisting a master. In addition, often the masters do not measure weights, volumes, or temperatures precisely. Needless to say, none of these brewers use a hydrometer.

I figured out the masters' recipes by interviewing the brewers and then deducing the missing details, such as water volumes. The brewers checked what I had written, and we together developed a sound recipe

The control panel of Sahtikrouvi, mounted in an old kuurna.

through several rounds of refinement. These brewers' actual batch volumes spanned a wide range, 60 to 200 liters, but I scaled each master's recipe to 25 US gallons (100 liters) to highlight the differences and similarities. Many of the original weights and volumes were nice round numbers or imprecise estimates, but the scaling and unit conversions have made some of the measurements here look more exact than they actually were.

An attentive brewer may notice that the water volumes in the masters' recipes are surprisingly low. This is because traditional kuurnas can be drained very dry: in a kuurna, four pounds of mash usually retains only around 1 quart (0.5 liters/kilogram) of water.

I use slightly different batch volumes for imperial and metric units, to provide for easy scaling between the units. The scaling is based on this approach: 2 pounds for 1 gallon gives the same weight-to-volume ratio as 1 kilogram for 4 liters. That enables a conversion in which 1 quart corresponds to 1 liter, 2 pounds to 1 kilogram, and 1 ounce to 30 grams. With this convention, a 5-gallon recipe corresponds to a 20-liter recipe, and 25 gallons to 100 liters.

Heikki Riutta's Sahti

Heikki Riutta is a farmer from the Finnish municipality of Sysmä who won the National Sahti Competition in 2006. In Sysmä they say "good sahti makes a thirst," and when I visited Heikki's farm I concluded that there's truth in that. Heikki brews in line with the family traditions taught to him by his father, and eventually he will pass on the brewing tradition to his sons.

Sysmä is in the barley-centric areas, where rye, especially dark rye malt, is more likely to be omitted from sahti. The barley-malt base enhances the fruity, spicy, and honeyish qualities of sahti. Lighter color and lower alcohol strength are also typical for the region.

Heikki's barley-only sahti exemplifies this sense of place well. He uses dark caramel malt to bring the color into the amber range, yet his ale is slightly paler than the average for sahtis. He prefers drinkability over strength, shooting for a "modest" 6 to 8 percent ABV. Heikki doesn't use any hops or juniper, which, in combination with the absence of dark rye malt, makes a very soft and rounded sahti. Without dark caramel malt, this sahti could be taken for a fairly typical Estonian koduõlu.

Heikki Riutta at his farmhouse brewery.

Heikki considers a long (eight- to nine-hour) mash step essential, insisting that sahti from a short mash will not taste the same. Usually he begins brewing at four o'clock in the morning, mashing in tandem with the farm work. He uses an electrically heated kettle, so he finds it convenient to add all the mash water at once instead of following the old wetting procedure. This is a raw ale with a maximum temperature of around 176°F (80°C).

Recipe for 25 gallons (100 liters)
74 lb. (37 kg) Sahti Malt
8 lb. (4 kg) caramel malt (100 EBC, or 40°L)
3.3 oz. (100 g) Finnish fresh compressed baker's yeast

Mix the malt into 19 gallons (75 liters) of 122°F (50°C) water, and let stand for two hours at 104 to 122°F (40 to 50°C). Raise the mash temperature to 140°F (60°C), and let rest for two hours. Over the next four hours, bring the temperature gradually to 176°F (80°C). Scoop the mash into a kuurna, and begin lautering when all the mash is in the kuurna. Recirculate the cloudy first wort back onto the mash. Toward the end of lautering, rinse the mash with boiling water until 25 gallons (100 liters) is collected.

Chill the wort to 73 to 77°F (23 to 25°C), and mix yeast into a small amount of wort. Whisk the wort while adding the yeast. Ferment at 59 to 68°F (15 to 20°C) for one to two days, and move the ale to canisters when the sahti is still slightly unfermented and sweet. Hold the canisters at around 59°F (15°C) for a day, and then cellar the ale. Close the containers loosely to prevent pressure from accumulating. This sahti is at its best when two weeks old.

Veli-Matti Heinonen's Sahti

In the municipality of Padasjoki, where Veli-Matti lives, sahti certainly feels like a well-defined beer style. In this part of sahti country, the local brewers unanimously prefer sweet and dark sahti containing around 10 percent dark rye malt. Another hallmark of the district is slow fermentation at lower temperatures.

Veli-Matti learned brewing from his mother in the 1980s, and the recipe hasn't changed much since, except for a few small refinements to the process and occasional experiments. He is a multiple sahti champion of Padasjoki, and in this province that is a noteworthy badge of honor.

Veli-Matti used to ferment his sahti in a root cellar where temperatures varied seasonally, in the range of 43–55°F (6–13°C), and the fer-

Veli-Matti Heinonen, a sahti master from Padasjoki.
COURTESY OF JYRKI VESA

mentation time varied accordingly, from four to six weeks. Now he has a dedicated cold room that stays at around 48°F (9°C), and fermentation takes one month. Most brewers who ferment in the cold wait for the yeast to become active in warm conditions, but Veli-Matti moves the wort to his cold room straight away, where fermentation begins after twenty-four hours.

Veli-Matti mashes with the traditional wetting method in a stainless steel kettle, and occasionally he heats the kettle to prevent sharp temperature drops during the eight to nine hours of mash time. He adds almost all the water to the mash, leaving only a little for sparging.

Juniper water is the only cleaning agent Veli-Matti uses in the brewery, and he even rinses plastic canisters with it. The recipe includes a special Finnish ingredient called *mämmimallas*, which in simple terms is pale rye malt flour intended for baking. Note that the way hops are applied is not a misprint—some sahti brewers actually rinse hops with hot water to reduce the bitterness they find harsh.

Recipe for 25 gallons (100 liters)
84 lb. (42 kg) Sahti Malt
10 lb. (5 kg) Kaljamallas (dark rye malt)
3.4 lb. (1.7 kg) mämmimallas (pale rye malt flour)
1.6 lb. (0.8 kg) rye flour (unmalted)
3.3 oz. (100 g) Finnish fresh compressed baker's yeast
Juniper branches for the lautering
Generous handful of whole hops

Pour the grains into a kettle, and mash with a four-step wetting procedure, using water that is (1) hand warm, (2) hot, (3) almost boiling, and (4) boiling. At each step, add 6.25 gallons (25 liters) of water, and then let the mash stand two hours. If necessary, heat the kettle to avoid large temperature drops. Finish mashing at around 176°F (80°C). Lay juniper branches at the bottom of the kuurna, and transfer the mash into it. Begin lautering, but pour the cloudy first wort back onto the mash. Rinse the mash with boiling water until 25 gallons (100 liters) is collected.

Transfer the wort into a kettle, and bring to a boil. Chill the wort to fermentation temperature: around 48°F (9°C). Put the hops in a bucket, and pour some boiling water over them. Then add the hop cones to the wort, discarding the water. Crumble yeast into the wort, and cover the fermenter loosely. Usually fermentation ramps up after twenty-four hours, and then the most active phase continues for three days. When the fermentation starts to calm down, scoop the sahti into canisters and sieve out the hop cones. Let the sahti ferment until the yeast has almost ceased its activity, which should take about one month. When ready, this sahti tastes fairly sweet and has a slight fizz.

The Sahti Academy's Rye Sahti

The municipalities of Isojoki and Honkajoki are in the stretch of western Finland known for passionate sahti brewers who are particularly fond of rye. Decades ago in this region, more than half of the grain bill was rye, but 30 to 40 percent is more typical today. That is still an impressive amount in comparison to most rye beers of the world.

In 2001 the brewers of the region established an association for their activities and built themselves a shared malt house and brewhouse. The name they chose for the facility was "Sahtiopisto," translated as "Sahti Academy," because the association's plan included offering courses in brewing sahti. In addition to teaching, it promotes the culture in various other ways. I got this recipe from the staff of the academy, which has earned plenty of medals in the National Sahti Competition with brews of this type. The recipe offers a good example of western Finnish rye sahti in general.

Several of the academy's members are farmers who grow, malt, and brew with their own rye. These days, the academy's brewers prefer malted rye, but occasionally they follow the old style and brew with unmalted rye. This recipe works with either malted or raw rye. As is characteristic of rye sahti, the mashing ends with boiling of the whole mash for at least half an hour.

> **Recipe for 25 gallons (100 liters)**
> 60 lb. (30 kg) Sahti Malt
> 40 lb. (20 kg) pale rye malt or unmalted rye
> 4 lb. (2 kg) Kaljamallas (dark rye malt)
> 3.3 oz. (100 g) Finnish fresh compressed baker's yeast
> Juniper branches for the lautering
> Small handful of whole hops (optional)

Sahti Academy director Hannu Väliviita showing guests the academy's brewhouse. An 80-gallon (300-liter) mashing kettle can be seen at the right and a stainless steel kuurna on the left.

Mash with the traditional five-step wetting procedure. At each step, add 6.25 gallons (25 liters) of water, letting the mash rest for two hours after every water addition. Begin with hand-warm water, use hot water at 140 to 176°F (60 to 80°C) for the second step, and perform the last three additions with boiling water. If necessary, heat the kettle to prevent dramatic temperature drops. After the last rest, boil the whole mash for half an hour to an hour.

Prepare the bottom of the kuurna with juniper branches, and transfer the mash into the kuurna. Begin lautering, but recirculate the cloudy first wort. Then collect every drop that comes from the kuurna—in this recipe the mash is not rinsed with water. While lautering, you may optionally prepare hops: boil the hops briefly in 1 quart (1 liter) of water, and then add the infusion containing hop cones to the wort.

Cool the wort to around 68°F (20°C), and mix yeast into a small amount of slightly cooled wort. Pitch the yeast, and ferment at 68 to 77°F (20 to 25°C) for one to two days, until the fermentation starts calming down. Move the sahti into storage canisters. If hops were used, sieve out the hop cones at this point. Place the canisters in a cellar, and mature the sahti in the cold for two weeks.

Paavo Pruul's Koduõlu

Paavo Pruul's surname actually means "brewing," and when I met him at his home brewery on the Estonian island of Hiiumaa, he was doing what that name obliges him to do. The name Pruul goes back five generations, to a man who worked as a brewer and distiller for a manor on the island. Paavo's traditional wooden brewing vats and brewing expertise come from his grandfather. When I visited, two boys under ten years of age were following their father attentively. I had no doubt that by manhood they'd have memorized all the details of brewing.

In the early 2010s, Paavo did the malting himself, but he had to abandon this approach when local barley suitable for malting became scarce. Also, he has gradually shifted from baker's yeast to brewer's yeast, which

Paavo Pruul & Sons brewing traditional Estonian koduõlu.

ferments in a more controllable manner. The hops he uses are homegrown. Paavo is accustomed to brewing without a thermometer. For example, he determines the mash water temperature by visually inspecting the water surface. When he does use a thermometer, it is mostly for checking the fermentation temperature.

Paavo's recipe varies with the season, and it is his summertime brew that I reproduce below. It contains less alcohol and more hops than his ales for colder times of year. Although Paavo uses slightly more juniper and hops than typical among koduõlu brewers, his õlu is a malt-forward and excellent example of sweet and soft Hiiumaa koduõlu.

His Christmas version is substantially stronger, with 100 pounds of malt for 25 gallons of ale (50 kilograms for 100 liters). Occasionally he flavors the Christmas ale with a few ounces of ground coffee added to the mash. In wintertime he may replace some of the hops with bog myrtle.

Paavo, also a keen hunter, has found a good use for the spent grains: he carries them into a forest to attract boars. After all, good meat and ale can work very well together.

Recipe for 25 gallons (100 liters)
66 lb. (33 kg) Vienna malt
1.7 oz. (50 g) Belgian-style dry yeast
Juniper branches for the lauter tun and one big branch for the
    juniper infusion
3 big handfuls of whole hops

Bring 33 gallons (130 liters) of water to a boil, add a big branch of juniper, and let infuse for two hours. Pour 10.5 gallons (42 liters) of this juniper infusion into a mash tun, and allow the water to cool to around 167°F (75°C). Mix in the malt, and let the mash tun rest, covered. Remove the juniper branch from the remaining infusion, add the hops, and boil the infusion for two hours. Then add 4 gallons (16 liters) of boiling juniper-hop infusion to the mash, and let stand for two more hours.

Scoop the mash into a lauter tun lined with juniper branches, and begin draining the wort. Pour the cloudy first wort back onto the grain bed, and then collect clear wort. When the mash surface level drops, rinse the mash with hot juniper-hop water to keep a thin layer of liquid visible above the mash. Stop collecting when you have 25 gallons (100 liters) of wort.

Cool the wort to 64 to 70°F (18 to 21°C), and add yeast. Let ferment for about two days, allowing the fermentation to begin slowing. You can monitor the progress with this handy old trick: Light a match just above the ale's surface. If carbon dioxide kills the flame, let the ale ferment further. Otherwise, transfer the ale into storage containers without delay, and move them into a cellar or similar space. Enjoy after two weeks of cold conditioning.

Homebrewer's Sahti

This is my standard sahti recipe adapted for typical homebrewing equipment. I have refined it on the basis of my tastes, various brewing experiments, and conversations with renowned sahti masters. Therefore, this is not a classic family recipe. Nevertheless, it provides a good example of Finnish homebrewed sahti today.

If you are already a homebrewer or a craft brewer, this recipe is an easy gateway to exploring raw farmhouse ales. I have included options for ingredients easily found outside Finland. I have also streamlined the

A sahti brew day in my yard. Usually I use the same brewing setup for both sahti and modern-style beers. COURTESY OF MARI VARONEN

mashing procedure, and with a heated mash tun the brew day can be over in less than five hours.

The recipe is written with either baker's yeast or kveik in mind, so I haven't included strict fermentation guidelines. Much depends on the particular yeast you have, but fermenting with baker's yeast at room temperature, 65 to 77°F (18 to 25°C), or with kveik at 86 to 104°F (30 to 40°C), is a good starting point. Ferment this with kveik and you'll get an exquisite farmhouse ale, though not a typical sahti for today's Finland.

Recipe for 5 gallons (20 liters)
Original gravity: 1.097 (23°P)
Final gravity: 1.034 (8.5°P)
Alcohol by volume: ~8 percent

14 lb. (7 kg) Pilsner or Vienna malt
4.8 lb. (2.4 kg) Munich malt
1.2 lb. (0.6 kg) Kaljamallas or caramel rye malt
0.8 oz. (24 g) fresh compressed baker's yeast, ⅓ oz. (10 g) dry
   baker's yeast, or kveik
0.4 oz. (12 g) juniper branches or juniper berries (optional)

Mash all the malt at 140°F (60°C) for forty-five minutes, using 1.1 quarts of water per pound of grains (2.3 liters/kilogram). If using juniper, mix the branches or berries into the mash. Raise the temperature to 158°F (70°C), hold at that temperature for forty-five minutes, and then raise to 176°F (80°C) for the final fifteen minutes. Begin lautering, and recirculate until the wort runs clear. Sparge with 176 to 194°F (80 to 90°C) water until 5 gallons (20 liters) of wort is collected. If using an immersion chiller, place it in the wort at the start of lautering to sterilize the chiller.

Chill the wort to fermentation temperature. If using baker's yeast, dissolve the fresh yeast in a small amount of cold water, or rehydrate dry yeast in 104°F (40°C) water. Pour the wort into the fermenter, add yeast, let ferment, and keep at fermentation temperature until the yeast is finishing its work. Depending on the yeast and temperature, this takes one to three days. When the sahti still tastes sweetish but is no longer cloying, move the fermenter into the cold. If unsure about the timing of this transfer, you can check whether the gravity is in the range 1.034–1.038.

Cold-condition the sahti for seven to ten days, and then rack into storage containers. The ale is ready immediately after racking. Store in cool conditions at all times.

Kitchen Sahti

This is an entry-level recipe that works without any dedicated brewing equipment. It yields a 1.5-gallon batch that can be brewed with fairly typical kitchen utensils and doesn't demand any prior brewing experience. You do need to obtain malt from a homebrew shop or a homebrewer friend, but that's pretty much it.

The recipe is designed around a stainless steel kettle large enough for the mash. The volume should be at least 10 quarts (10 liters), and a 12-quart stockpot would be perfect for the job. You'll also need a lautering vessel of the same size, which could, for example, involve a bucket, hose, and copper pipe, as described on page 168. A kitchen colander is a passable option too.

To minimize the equipment requirements, I advocate the old farmhouse trick: use the mashing vat—the kettle in this case—as a fermenter. Beverage dispensers or plastic PET bottles are the easiest containers for storing the ale. Glass bottles too can be used, if pressure buildup can be prevented. A homebrewing racking cane (a hard plastic tube for siphoning) would make transferring sahti from one vessel to another easier.

The recipe is written for my simple and effective mashing procedure, but once you learn the techniques with a thermometer, you can start experimenting with other techniques as well. This kind of small batch does mean relatively large losses to dregs, and the final yield is around 4 or 5 quarts (or liters) of fairly sediment-free ale.

> **Recipe for 1.5 gallons (6 liters)**
> 6 lb. (3 kg) Vienna or Pilsner malt
> 0.4 lb. (0.2 kg) caramel rye malt
> Small juniper twig or 2 g juniper berries (optional)
> Level teaspoon of dry baker's yeast

Heat 6.5 quarts (6.5 liters) of water in the kettle, to 150°F (66°C), and mix in the crushed malt. If using juniper, add the twig or berries to the

With some inventiveness, sahti can be brewed in virtually every kitchen. Here, a household kettle is used for mashing and a steam juicer for lautering.

mash at this point. Keep the mash above 140°F (60°C) for forty-five minutes. You may need to heat the mash occasionally. If the kettle fits in the oven, heating it there is a convenient way to maintain this temperature. Heat the mash to 158°F (70°C), and hold at this temperature for forty-five minutes. Finally, heat the mash to 176°F (80°C), keeping it there for fifteen minutes.

Scoop the mash into a lautering vessel, and let the wort flow into a temporary storage vessel set aside for it. Meanwhile, clean the kettle of visible material. Once the kettle is clean, pour the cloudy wort you have collected onto the mash, and let clear wort flow from the lautering vessel into the kettle. Finally, rinse the mash with 3 quarts (3 liters) of boiling water. Collect all the wort—the mash should have no remaining liquid.

Cool the wort in the kettle to around 68°F (20°C), and then sprinkle the yeast onto the wort. Let the sahti ferment at 65 to 77°F (18 to 25°C) until fermentation begins to slow. The sahti should still taste sweet.

Usually this takes one to three days. Pour or rack the sahti into storage containers, leaving the majority of the sediment behind. Move the containers to a space at 32 to 50°F (0 to 10°C), and let mature for a week or two. To prevent gushing, close the containers only loosely or check the pressure occasionally.

Late-Runnings Ale

Traditionally, late runnings from sahti mash have been fermented into a low-alcohol kalja or ladies' sahti. Since the late runnings depend a lot on how the sahti is made, there are no exact recipes for this kind of ale, but there are some guidelines.

As the rinsing of the mash continues, the gravity and quality of the late runnings decrease constantly. It seems that the typical volume for late-runnings kalja in the past was one to one-and-a-half times that of the sahti. That would have been a very weak ale indeed, and if you want

Sahti master Seppo Lisma collects late runnings for a quarter of the volume of his sahti batch. This late-runnings ale is fermented much like sahti but served on everyday occasions before the feast. MIKA LAITINEN

to try this yourself, I suggest collecting no more than half the volume of the sahti batch itself. The first quarter of the volume is probably of considerable gravity and fit for ladies' sahti, a feast ale that should have a rich and sweet taste but no more than a few percent alcohol.

Whether the goal is kalja or ladies' sahti, late-runnings ales are typically fermented very briefly, mainly to preserve the ale. Fermentation is started with a tiny amount of the yeast used for the sahti, traditionally "a pinch." Those who want a more concrete descriptor can try, for example, one fifth of the amount used for the sahti itself. Skimping on yeast will restrain fermentation.

Another trick is to retard fermentation by moving the ale into the cold early. Usually the fermentation at room temperature takes less than ten hours. In the cold, yeast usually produces a little fizz before coming to a halt, which adds a refreshing touch. Again, slow fermentation may continue in the cold, so the containers may need to be monitored. Since less yeast is used, the ale will not be very yeasty, and it should be ready to drink within two days. Kalja and ladies' sahti were rarely given additional flavoring, but a small amount of juniper berries or dry hops added to the fermenter as an accent can enhance the taste nicely.

Late runnings also offer a great canvas for experimental brews. For example, the late runnings from unboiled sahti wort make for an excellent Berliner weisse–style ale—just cool the wort, add yeast and lactic bacteria, and proceed as you normally would with a Berliner weisse.

Søhti

On occasion I brew sahti wort but then freewheel with the fermentation. For example, I pitch brewer's yeast and bottle-condition the ale. I brew these ales simply because I like the flavor, not to follow any tradition. The fresh taste of raw ale is marvelous, though the resulting beverage doesn't last for months. Also, this type of ale offers an easy gateway to the old brewing techniques.

Since the brews I'll describe here aren't exactly traditional, I have begun to refer to them by the word *søhti*, using a Scandinavian ø character because I have often brewed them with yeast obtained from my friends in Norway and Denmark—either kveik or another yeast hunted down locally.

This technique works for a wide variety of yeasts. American and British ale yeast leave more room for fresh maltiness, while Belgian or French farmhouse ale yeast brings out the rustic qualities. A weizen yeast produces a flavor quite close to that of sahti. The following recipe is written for a yeast that does not contain souring bacteria, but raw ale wort is a good base for sour ales too.

The recipe below is only one example of this method; consider it a starting point. Because this ale ferments drier than sahti, I prefer to drop the original gravity to the 15 to 20°P range. With the hop tea method, this recipe makes a great hopped raw ale too. In fact, if you lower the gravity to around 1.061 (15°P), leave out the rye malt, and replace the juniper with 2 or 3 ounces of low-alpha-acid hops, you'll end up with a raw ale approaching the Lithuanian kaimiškas style.

Recipe for 5 gallons (20 liters)
Original gravity: 1.083 (20°P)
Final gravity: 1.022 (5.6°P)
Alcohol by volume: 8 percent

13.2 lb. (6.6 kg) Vienna malt
0.8 lb. (0.4 kg) Kaljamallas or caramel rye malt
0.4 oz. (12 g) juniper branches or 2 to 3 oz. (60 to 90 g) whole
    hops of your choice
Brewer's yeast or kveik devoid of bacteria

Make the wort as in the "Homebrewer's Sahti" recipe. If using juniper branches, add half of them to the mash, and put the other half in the wort while lautering. If you opt to use hops, brew the hop tea as advised on page 174.

Chill the wort to fermentation temperature, and pitch the yeast. Ferment to completion, and cellar the ale without delay. Keg or bottle as soon as most of the yeast has flocculated. If kegging, I recommend shooting for smooth carbonation (2.0 to 2.5 volumes of carbon dioxide). If bottling, prime with sugar and bottle-condition in a warm environment until sufficiently carbonated—add around 3 ounces of sugar for 4.5 gallons of finished ale (5 grams/liter). Cold storage isn't absolutely necessary, but it will preserve the freshness longer.

Medieval or Viking Ale

This is a shape-shifting recipe suitable for brewing various kinds of historical unhopped ales. The general brewing process for a sahti-like ale is relatively fixed, while the recipes travel in space and time through the choice of grains, herbs, and yeast.

I provided the background for the ingredient selection in the chapter "Re-creating Medieval and Viking Ales." Here, I'll give several options for gruit ales, medieval English ales, and Viking ales. Consider these recipe variants merely starting points.

By medieval standards, these would almost certainly be feast ales or the finest ales of well-to-do people. I believe the gravity and alcohol content for the general recipe would have been near the upper end of the range a thousand years ago. If you want to experience an everyday medieval ale, brew a weaker ale from the late runnings.

I have omitted specific yeast recommendations because the type of yeast is not the most important matter with regard to historical accuracy. The main question is how primitive a yeast you are willing to handle.

This kind of brewing equipment certainly looks cool in a historic brewing demonstration, but medieval or Viking Age brewing processes can be easily realized with standard homebrewing equipment as well. COURTESY OF SAMI BRODKIN

Choose the yeast to match your skills, your ambitions, and the amount of effort you want to put into these re-creations, as discussed in the chapter "Re-creating Medieval and Viking Ales" (page 191).

The modern measurements below are meant to assist you, but you can gradually learn to brew without them if you want to reenact the whole process: measure malt by volume, and replace the two-step mash described below with the traditional thermometer-free wetting procedure.

Recipe for 5 gallons (20 liters)
Original gravity: 1.075 (18°P)
Final gravity: 1.019 to 1.028 (4.8 to 7.1°P)
Alcohol by volume: 6 to 7 percent

12.8 lb. (6.4 kg) of malt and unmalted grains of your choice
Brewing herbs of your choice
Yeast of your choice

These are my favorite options, to get you started:

Gruit Ale
8 lb. (4 kg) Vienna or pale ale malt
2.4 lb. (1.2 kg) smoked malt
2.4 lb. (1.2 kg) Munich malt
0.67 oz. (20 g) dried bog myrtle *or* 0.25 oz. (7.5 g) fresh
   rosemary and 0.33 oz. (10 g) fresh sage

Medieval English Ale
6 lb. (3 kg) pale ale malt
2.4 lb. (1.2 kg) smoked malt
2.4 lb. (1.2 kg) Munich malt
2 lb. (1 kg) oat malt or oat flakes
No brewing herbs *or* 0.67 oz. (20 g) dried ground ivy
   (*Glechoma hederacea*)

Viking Ale
6.4 lb. (3.2 kg) Vienna malt
6.4 lb. (3.2 kg) smoked malt
One of these herbs: 0.67 oz. (20 g) fresh juniper branches,
   0.67 oz. (20 g) dried bog myrtle, *or* 0.67 oz. (20 g) dried
   yarrow

The brewing process is the same for all of these ingredient choices.

Mash at 149 to 158°F (65 to 70°C) for two hours, using 4 gallons (16 liters) of water. If using herbs, add half of them to the mash along with the grains. Raise the mash to 167 to 176°F (75 to 80°C), and hold at this temperature for half an hour. Begin lautering, and recirculate until the wort runs clear. If using herbs, add the other half of them to the wort (putting them in a cloth bag should make things easier). Sparge with water around 176°F (80°C) until 5 gallons (20 liters) of wort are collected. If using an immersion chiller, insert it at the beginning of lautering so that the hot wort sterilizes it.

Chill the wort to fermentation temperature, and pull out the herbs from the wort. Add the yeast of your choice. You may either ferment this like sahti, cellaring the ale when fermentation becomes subdued, or let the ale finish fermenting in warm conditions and then move the fermenter to the cold promptly.

Rack the ale into its final containers when most of the yeast has flocculated. This ale should be ready to drink within a week or two. For carbonation, apply the same principles as with sahti: still ale or a smooth fizz from residual fermentation would be authentic. If taking a slightly more relaxed stance on the tradition, you may inject CO_2 when kegging or prime with a small amount of sugar.

A REVIEW OF REFERENCES AND BIBLIOGRAPHY

I WANTED TO WRITE AN EASYGOING BOOK, so I chose to avoid numbered citations. Another reason for ditching the good old footnote/endnote system is that many of my sources are either written in Nordic languages such as Finnish or otherwise inaccessible to most readers. Besides, a large quantity of the data comes from my own experience and didn't exist in written form before this book. Nevertheless, a book entirely ignoring the sources would be very frustrating, and I'll try to make up for that in a practical way here.

Except in works by a few great ethnographers, domestic northern folk ales haven't been a popular topic to write about. So I've had to scrape small bits of information from various sources. Some of these are not scientific references but from blogs and other nonscientific sources I consider trustworthy. In fact, the picture the literature paints of folk ales would be quite one-dimensional without diligent hobbyists, and the same applies to parts of beer history.

Sahti Road Trips and Finnish Ethnographic Texts

I have been brewing sahti and meeting sahti masters since 2005, but my understanding of the craft grew most significantly in 2014–2015, when I collected data for the Finnish book *Sahtikirja* (2015) with Johannes Silvennoinen and Hannu Nikulainen. We met more than fifty sahti brewers and tasted at least a hundred sahtis. This journey took us to both home-based and commercial breweries, and we brewed with some of the masters. As we experienced the living culture, we also heard amazing stories of the past, with the oldest ones going back to the 1940s. This, coupled with dozens of brewing experiments at my home brewery, formed the bulk of the source material for this book.

My major references for sahti traditions of the past were Matti Räsänen's PhD thesis "Vom Halm zum Fass" (a 1975 work written, somewhat surprisingly, in German), Carl Niclas Hellenius's thesis "Finska allmogens bryggnings-sätt" (from 1780, in Swedish), and *Sahtikirja* (a 1990 book edited by Ulla Asplund).

Räsänen's extremely well-researched ethnographic monograph was based on surveys carried out in 1933, 1958, and 1967. These involved questionnaires that

Second only to the winter solstice, the summer solstice marks a major seasonal festival for sahti folks, and the classic place to celebrate it is beside a lake. Finland is often referred to as the land of a thousand lakes, but officially there are closer to 188,000 of them.

also covered the culture of decades earlier, extending back to the turn of the century. Räsänen's work addresses mostly ingredients, the brewing process, equipment, and etymology. *Sahtikirja*, in turn, is a collection of stories obtained from traditional brewers. It represents almost the only written account of old-time farmhouse malting in Finland. In the chapter on history, the etymology of sahti and Finnish brewing vocabulary strongly echo the work of Räsänen.

The foundation for insight into traditional Finnish farmhouse life was laid by books by distinguished ethnographers: Uuno Sirelius's *Suomen kansanomaista kulttuuria I* (1919), Toivo Vuorela's *Suomalainen kansankulttuuri* (1975), and one work actually available in English—Ilmar Talve's *Finnish Folk Culture* (2012). The books *Viinan voima* (2001), by folklorist Satu Apo, and *Juomareiden valtakunta* (2015), by historian Kustaa H. J. Vilkuna, shed light on the role of alcohol in Finnish farmhouse life.

My knowledge of eastern Finnish low-alcohol farmhouse ales was based mostly on Räsänen's thesis, the ethnographic works mentioned above, and Karelian cookbooks (by Räsänen, Aino Lampinen, Pirkko Sallinen-Gimpi, and Irja Seppänen-Pora). The incredible story of collecting boar's saliva to get ale fermentation started was found in Uno Harva's *Suomalaisten muinaisusko* (1948).

The Other Northern Farmhouse Ales

My knowledge of koduõlu is based largely on a tour of the Estonian islands in 2015. I met eight brewers, with the assistance of local guide Mattias Hiiumaal. Additional background information was provided by Tormis Jakovlev's koduõlu booklet "Olut Virossa" (1995, in Finnish), and Gustav Ränk's ethnographic book *Vanha Viro: Kansa ja kulttuuri* (1955, a Finnish translation of an Estonian work). Lars Marius Garshol's blog entries and Martin Thibault's article "Breaking Bread with Seto Õlu" on the BeerAdvocate website shed light on oven beers of Setomaa.

The main source addressing gotlandsdricke was Anders Salomonsson's classic *Gotlandsdricka: Traditionell kultur som regional identitetssymbol* (1979, in Swedish). This well-researched book from forty years ago was supplemented with newer information from Garshol's blog, Charlie Papazian's visit to Gotland as documented in *Microbrewed Adventures*, Svante Ekelin's take on the topic in *The Oxford Companion to Beer*, and the news website helagotland.se.

For maltøl I followed the classic text by Odd Nordland *Brewing and Beer Traditions in Norway* (1969) and the recent Garshol book *Gårdsøl: Det norske ølet* (2016, in Norwegian). Garshol's blog was another extremely valuable source in this regard. To meet Norwegian farmhouse maltsters and brewers in person, I went on a road trip to Stjørdal and Hornindal in summer 2017.

As for Lithuanian farmhouse ales, I refer to Garshol's work, specifically his blog and the book *Lithuanian Beer: A Rough Guide*. The flavors and lesser-known facts about kaimiškas brewing practices became evident to me on a pub crawl in Vilnius and from a two-hour chat with local brewmaster and folk beer expert Simonas Gutautas.

Michael Jackson toured Nordic and Baltic farmhouse breweries in the 1990s, and some of these adventures were documented on his website Beer Hunter. Finnish beer writer Unto Tikkanen, who traveled with him in Finland and the Baltic countries, captured the travels from a different angle in his book *Viinin ja oluen lähteillä* (2004, in Finnish). This book provided great insight into the Baltic ales just after the collapse of the Iron Curtain and how Jackson viewed the farmhouse culture.

Phil Markowski's *Farmhouse Ales* was an invaluable source of material on Belgian and French farmhouse ales. During the writing process, the debate over the farmhouse origin of saisons culminated in Roel Mulder's blog post "Fact Check: Yvan De Baets on Saison" (2018), which included an illuminating comment from De Baets himself.

As of 2018, Russian farmhouse ales and kvass-type cereal beverages are still little documented in the Western world, especially when it comes to more traditional versions. Again, Garshol's expedition to Russia and the stories on his blog filled in the gap to some extent. The article "Microbial and Chemical Analysis of a Kvass Fermentation" (2008), by Elena Dlusskaya et al., provided a picture of kvass today.

The boza of the Balkans, Turkey, and Egypt is reasonably well documented, but since this more southern ale represented clearly a more distant side path for me, I didn't spent much time researching the drink. The understanding of boza was based primarily on Penka Petrova and Kaloyan Petrov's article "Traditional Cereal Beverage Boza" (2017), along with the book *Ancient Egyptian Materials and Industries* (1962), by A. Lucas and J. R. Harris.

Archaeology and History

The view on early farming in the North was formed mainly by two massive tomes on archaeology: *Ancient Scandinavia* (2015), by T. Douglas Price, and *Muinaisuutemme jäljet* (2015), on archaeology of Finland, by Georg Haggrén and colleagues. Useful insight was provided by Santeri Vanhanen and Satu Koivisto's article "Pre-Roman Iron Age Settlement Continuity and Cereal Cultivation in Coastal Finland as Shown by Multiproxy Evidence at Bäljars 2 Site in SW Finland" (2015), which presented archaeobotanical evidence that Finns were already utilizing juniper two thousand years ago, though we don't know whether the efforts back then were for beer.

The treatment of early mixed fermented drinks followed Patrick McGovern's book *Uncorking the Past* (2009) and the article "A Biomolecular Archaeological Approach to 'Nordic Grog'" (2013), by McGovern and colleagues.

Merryn Dineley's account on neolithic malting and brewing in Scotland was from the paper "Neolithic Ale" (2000). Archaeological evidence related to beer in neolithic and Bronze Age Scotland is discussed in Max Nelson's book *The Barbarian's Beverage* (2005) as well.

The Barbarian's Beverage was the main source of material on brewing in northern Europe during the Bronze Age and Iron Age. This book contains several excerpts in which Roman historians describe Germanic and Celtic beer culture of the first millennium. The archaeological evidence of malting in northern Europe was selected from Nelson's article "The Geography of Beer in Europe from 1000 BC to AD 1000" (2014). Fascinating newer information on Iron Age malting was provided by Mikael Larsson et al. in the article "Botanical Evidence of Malt for Beer Production in Fifth–Seventh Century Uppåkra, Sweden" (2018).

A lot has been written about the Vikings, but the information on their drinks and drinking culture is scattered with vast numbers of tiny clues. In the chapter "History of Farmhouse Ales" I referred to *Orkneyinga Saga* (1980, translated by H. Pálsson and P. Edwards), *The Poetic Edda* (2014, translated by C. Larrington), and the writings of Adam of Bremen from *History of the Archbishops of Hamburg-Bremen* (2002, translated by F. J. Tschan with an introduction by T. Reuter). Merryn and Graham Dineley provided an archaeological view in their article "Where Were the Viking Brew Houses?" (2013). The idea that mead wasn't the most common feast drink of the Vikings was supported by Garshol's blog article "Mead: A Norwegian Tradition?" (2018).

Many more, similar references exist. An excellent survey on beer, mead, and wine in Viking culture can be found in James Buckley's master's thesis "Inspiration and Inebriation: Transformative Drinks in Old Norse Literature" (2015). For those interested in how feasting with food and drink was woven into the Vikings' culture, I recommend these books: *The Age of the Vikings* (2014), by Anders Winroth; *The Vikings* (2018), by Else Roesdahl; and *An Early Meal: A Viking Age Cookbook & Culinary Odyssey* (2013), by Daniel Serra and Hanna Tunberg.

The essential references for medieval ales were Richard W. Unger's book *Beer in the Middle Ages and the Renaissance* (2007), Judith Bennett's *Ale, Beer, and Brewsters in England* (1996), and Martyn Cornell's *Beer: The Story of the Pint* (2003). My presentation of the evolution of hopped beer largely followed these books, along with Cornell's blog article "A Short History of Hops" (2009).

The main sources of information on gruit ales were Roel Mulder's article "Further Notes on the Essence of Gruit: An Alternative View" (2017) and his blog piece "Gruit: Nothing Mysterious About It" (2017), along with Susan Verberg's "The Rise and Fall of Gruit" (2018). Cornell's book *Amber, Gold & Black* (2010) and his blog article "Was It Ever Gruit in Britain? The Herb Ale Tradition" (2014) cast some light on historical herbal and unhopped ales in the British Isles.

In the chapter "Re-creating Medieval and Viking Ales," the account of bog myrtle and yarrow as medieval Nordic brewing herbs was based mostly on Nordland's *Brewing and Beer Traditions in Norway*. An article titled "Viking Age Garden Plants from Southern Scandinavia" (2012), by Pernille R. Sloth et al., prompted the question "did the Vikings brew with hops?"

In the chapter on history, the musings on omitting the wort boil were backed up by Franz G. Meussdoerffer's "A Comprehensive History of Beer Brewing" (2009) and Cornell's *Beer: The Story of the Pint*. Geir Grønnesby wrote an article on boiling with stones (2016's "Hot Rocks! Beer Brewing on Viking and Medieval Age Farms in Trøndelag") that provided valuable background information as well. Olaus Magnus's fascinating observations from the early sixteenth-century Nordic countries, on brewing and fermentation in particular, were extracted from *A Description of the Northern Peoples* (1996, translated by P. Fisher and H. Higgins).

In the chapter "Low-Alcohol Farmhouse Ales," the ancient beer recipe by Greek alchemist Zosimus came from *The Barbarian's Beverage*. Also, this book provided a critical review of what we know of the beers of the ancient Middle East, Egypt in particular. Another critical, if not downright skeptical, account on ancient ales was found in Peter Damerow's "Sumerian Beer: The Origins of Brewing Technology in Ancient Mesopotamia" (2012).

Brewing Science and Botany

The scientific expertise in beer ingredients is largely grounded in Brewers Publications books: *Malt*, by John Mallet (2012); *Yeast* (2010), by Chris White and Jamil Zainasheff; and *For the Love of Hops* (2012), by Stan Hieronymus. In addition, Wolgang Kunze's *Technology Brewing and Malting* (1999) and John Palmer's *How to Brew* (2017) were important references addressing modern malting and brewing processes.

In the chapter "Drinking Sahti," the chemical analysis of sahti relied on an article by Jukka Ekberg and colleagues, "Physicochemical Characterization of Sahti, an 'Ancient' Beer Style Indigenous to Finland" (2015).

The sections of this book dealing with the ancient fermentation and domestication of yeasts referred to an article by Brigida Gallone et al., "Domestication and Divergence of *Saccharomyces cerevisiae* Beer Yeasts" (2016). This paper presented a genetic family tree for hundreds of commercial yeasts but did not include domestic farmhouse yeasts. Norwegian kveiks were added to the tree in the article "Traditional Norwegian Kveik Are a Genetically Distinct Group of Domesticated *Saccharomyces cerevisiae* Brewing Yeasts" (2018), by Richard Preiss et al. With these fascinating and groundbreaking articles, we have only begun to understand where our yeast came from.

To obtain information on Sahti Malt, I visited Viking Malt in Lahti. I also interviewed a yeast specialist from Suomen Hiiva, the producer of the typical sahti yeast. The information on commercial sahti ingredients was supplemented with the histories of the yeast and malt companies as offered in books by Olavi Latikka, Kari Leinamo, and Olli Vehviläinen.

A few interesting details about Finnish baker's yeast were obtained from the blog *Suregork Loves Beer*, by Kristoffer Krogerus (one of the scientists behind the "Physicochemical Characterization of Sahti . . ." paper) and from the master's thesis of Marjo Leinonen, "Sahdin hiivaus ja aistinvarainen arviointi" (2009), containing sensory comparisons of sahtis fermented with various baker's yeasts.

I am fortunate that my local university is home to a specialist in native Finnish wild plants, University of Jyväskylä biologist Minna-Maarit Kytöviita. She shared many interesting facts about the flavors of juniper, but, regrettably, reports on flavor differences between male and female plants have not been published. For other wild brewing herbs—such as yarrow, bog myrtle, and ground ivy—my main source was the well-researched Finnish website NatureGate, with content in English as well.

Practical Tips on Brewing

Recommending further reading for homebrewers makes me uneasy, since modern brewing textbooks tend to distract from traditional brewing. Nevertheless, such books can be highly useful—for example, when one is buying or building brewing equipment. Just be ready to turn a blind eye to some of the modern rules! My favorite classic brewing guidebooks of today are Palmer's *How to Brew* (2017) and Randy Mosher's *Mastering Homebrew* (2015). For Finnish brewers, I would, of course, recommend my own homebrewing book, *Rakkaudella pantua* (2016). Jereme Zimmerman's recent guidebook *Brew Beer Like a Yeti* (2018) is actually geared toward traditional brewing techniques. Finally, the guide *Small-Scale Brewing* (1997), written by Finnish brewmaster Ilkka Sysilä, includes a section on brewing sahti and instructions for hollowing out your kuurna.

Foraging for brewing herbs has become popular in the latter part of the 2010s, and now we have several books that are useful for finding and using historic brewing herbs. Examples are Hieronymus's *Brewing Local* (2016) and *The Homebrewer's Almanac* (2016), by Marika Josephson et al.

Bibliography

Adam of Bremen. *History of the Archbishops of Hamburg–Bremen*. Translated by Francis Joseph Tschan. New York: Columbia University Press, 2002.

Ahola, J., Frog, and Jenni Lucenius, eds. *The Viking Age in Åland*. Helsinki: Suomalaisen tiedeakatemian toimituksia, 2014.

Alenius, Teija, Teemu Mökkönen, and Antti Lahelma. "Early Farming in the Northern Boreal Zone: Reassessing the History of Land Use in Southeastern Finland Through High-Resolution Pollen Analysis." *Geoarchaeology* 28, no. 1 (2013): 1–24.

Apo, Satu. *Viinan voima: Näkökulmia suomalaisten kansanomaiseen alkoholiajatteluun ja -kulttuuriin*. Helsinki: Finnish Literature Society, 2001.

Asplund, Ulla, ed. *Sahti: Kaskuja ja tarinoita*. Lammi, Finland: Suomen Sahtiseura, 1993.

———. *Sahtikirja*. Lammi, Finland: Suomen Sahtiseura, 1990.

Behre, Karl-Ernst. "The History of Beer Additives in Europe—a Review." *Vegetation History and Archaeobotany* 8, no. 1–2 (June 1999): 35–48.

Bennett, Judith M. *Ale, Beer and Brewsters in England: Women's Work in a Changing World, 1300–1600*. New York: Oxford University Press, 1996.

Buckley, James. "Inspiration and Inebriation: Transformative Drinks in Old Norse Literature." Master's thesis, University of Cambridge, 2015.

Cornell, Martyn. *Amber, Gold & Black: The History of Britain's Great Beers*. Charleston, SC: The History Press, 2010.

———. "A Short History of Hops." *Zythophile* (blog), November 20, 2009. http://zythophile.co.uk/2009/11/20/a-short-history-of-hops/.

———. *Beer: The Story of the Pint*. London: Headline Book Publishing, 2003.

———. "Was It Ever Gruit in Britain? The Herb Ale Tradition." *Zythophile* (blog), February 28, 2014. http://zythophile.co.uk/2014/02/28/was-it-ever -gruit-britain-the-herb-ale-tradition/.

Damerow, Peter. "Sumerian Beer: The Origins of Brewing Technology in Ancient Mesopotamia." *Cuneiform Digital Library Journal* 2012, no. 2.

Dineley, Graham, and Merryn Dineley. "Where Were the Viking Brew Houses?" *EXARC Journal* 2013, no. 2. https://exarc.net/issue-2013-2/ea/where-were -viking-brew-houses.

Dineley, Merryn. "Neolithic Ale: Barley as a Source of Sugars for Fermentation." In *Plants in Neolithic Britain and Beyond*, edited by Andrew S. Fairbairn, 137–153. Oxford: Oxbow Books, 2000.

Dlusskaya, Elena, André Jänsch, Clarissa Schwab, and Michael G. Gänzle. "Microbial and Chemical Analysis of a Kvass Fermentation." *European Food Research and Technology* 227, no. 1 (2008): 261–266.

Ekberg, J., B. Gibson, J. Joensuu, K. Krogerus, F. Magalhães, A. Mikkelson, T. Seppänen-Laakso, and A. Wilpola. "Physicochemical Characterization of Sahti, an 'Ancient' Beer Style Indigenous to Finland." *Journal of the Institute of Brewing* 121, no. 4 (September 2015): 464–473.

Ekelin, Svante. "Sweden." In *The Oxford Companion to Beer*, edited by Garrett Oliver, 777–779. New York: Oxford University Press, 2012.

European Commission, Agriculture and Rural Development. "TSG-appellation of Sahti." Appellation registered February 2002, http://ec.europa .eu/agriculture/quality/door (search with the keyword "sahti").

Gallone, B., J. Steensels, T. Prahl, L. Soriaga, V. Saels, B. Herrera-Malaver, et al. "Domestication and Divergence of *Saccharomyces cerevisiae* Beer Yeasts." *Cell* 166, no. 6 (September 2016): 1397–1410.

Garshol, Lars Marius. *Gårdsøl: Det norske ølet*. Oslo: Cappelen Damm, 2016.

———. *Lithuanian Beer: A Rough Guide*. Self-published e-book, 2014. www.garshol.priv.no/download/lithuanian-beer-guide/book.pdf.

———. "Mead: A Norwegian Tradition?" *Larsblog* (blog), April 15, 2018. www.garshol.priv.no/blog/387.html.

———. "Oven Beer in Central Russia," *Larsblog* (blog), November 7, 2018. www.garshol.priv.no/blog/398.html.

———. "Was All Beer Sour Before Pasteur?" *Larsblog* (blog), October 26, 2014. www.garshol.priv.no/blog/306.html.

Grønnesby, Geir. "Hot Rocks! Beer Brewing on Viking and Medieval Age Farms in Trøndelag." In *The Agrarian Life of the North 2000 BC–AD 1000: Studies in Rural Settlement and Farming in Norway*, edited by Frode Iversen and Håkan Petersson, 133–149. Oslo: Cappelen Damm Akademisk, 2017.

Haggrén, Georg, Petri Halinen, Mika Lavento, Sami Raninen, and Anna Wessman. *Muinaisuutemme jäljet: Suomen esi- ja varhaishistoria kivikaudelta keskiajalle*. Helsinki: Gaudeamus Helsinki University Press, 2015.

Harva, Uno. *Suomalaisten muinaisusko*. Helsinki: WSOY, 1948.

Hellenius, Carl Niclas. "Finska allmogens bryggnings-sätt." Dissertation, Royal Academy of Turku, 1780. Digitized by the National Library of Finland. http://urn.fi/urn:nbn:fi:fv-12541.

Hieronymus, Stan. *Brewing Local: American-Grown Beer*. Boulder, CO: Brewers Publications, 2016.

———. *For the Love of Hops: The Practical Guide to Aroma, Bitterness and the Culture of Hops*. Boulder, CO: Brewers Publications, 2012.

Jackson, Michael. Beer Hunter (website). www.beerhunter.com/beerhunting.html.

———. *The World Guide to Beer*. London: Mitchell Beazley, 1977.

Jakovlev, Tormis. *Olut Virossa*. Tampere, Finland: Tampereen museot, 1995.

Josephson, Marika, Aaron Kleidon, and Ryan Tockstein. *The Homebrewer's Almanac: A Seasonal Guide to Making Your Own Beer from Scratch*. New York: Countryman Press, 2016.

Klemettilä, Hannele. *The Medieval Kitchen: A Social History with Recipes*. London: Reaktion Books, 2012.

Korpinen, Santtu, and Hannu Nikulainen. *Suomalaiset pienpanimot*. Jyväskylä, Finland: Kirjakaari, 2014.

Krogerus, Kristoffer. "Physiology of Finnish Baker's Yeast." *Suregork Loves Beer* (blog), August 28, 2014. http://beer.suregork.com/?p=3514.

Kunze, Wolfgang. *Technology Brewing and Malting*. Berlin: VLB Berlin, 1999.

Lampinen, Aino. *Karjalainen keittokirja*. Joensuu, Finland: Karjalaisen kulttuurin edistämiskeskus, 1978.

Larrington, Carolyne, trans. *The Poetic Edda*. Oxford: Oxford University Press, 2014.

Larsson, Mikael, Andreas Svensson, and Jan Apel. "Botanical Evidence of Malt for Beer Production in Fifth–Seventh Century Uppåkra, Sweden." *Archaeological and Anthropological Sciences* 2018. https://doi.org/10.1007/s12520-018-0642-6

Latikka, Olavi. *Lahtelaisen hiivateollisuuden vaiheet 1897–1997: Suomen Hiiva Oy—perinteitä ja yhteistyötä*. Lahti, Finland: Suomen Hiiva, 1997.

Leinamo, Kari. *Puhtaasti viljasta: Laihian Mallas Oy 1910–2010*. Laihia, Finland: Laihian Mallas, 2010.

Leinonen, Marjo. "Sahdin hiivaus ja aistinvarainen arviointi." Master's thesis, Häme University of Applied Sciences, 2009.

Lönnrot, Elias, ed. *Kalevala*. Helsinki: Otava, 2012. The work was originally published in 1849; several translations are currently available in English.

Magnus, Olaus. *A Description of the Northern Peoples, 1555, Vol. 1 (Historia de gentibus septentrionalibus)*. Edited by Peter Foote and translated by Peter Fisher and Humphrey Higgins. London: Hakluyt Society, 1996.

Mallet, John. *Malt: A Practical Guide from Field to Brewhouse*. Boulder, CO: Brewers Publications, 2014.

Markowski, Phil. *Farmhouse Ales: Culture and Craftsmanship in the Belgian Tradition*. Boulder, CO: Brewers Publications, 2004.

McGovern, Patrick E. *Uncorking the Past: The Quest for Wine, Beer, and Other Alcoholic Beverages*. Berkeley, CA: University of California Press, 2009.

McGovern, Patrick E., Gretchen R. Hall, and Armen Mirzoian. "A Biomolecular Archaeological Approach to 'Nordic Grog.'" *Danish Journal of Archaeology* 2, no. 2 (2013): 112–131.

Meussdoerffer, Franz G. "A Comprehensive History of Beer Brewing." In *Handbook of Brewing: Processes, Technology, Markets*, edited by Hans M. Eßlinger, 1–42. Weinheim, Germany: Wiley-VCH, 2009.

Mosher, Randy. *Mastering Homebrew: The Complete Guide to Brewing Delicious Beer*. San Francisco: Chronicle Books, 2015.

Mulder, Roel. "Fact check: Yvan De Baets on Saison." *Lost Beers* (blog), October 31, 2018. http://lostbeers.com/fact-check-yvan-de-baets-on-saison-and-the -results-may-shock-you/.

———. "Further Notes on the Essence of Gruit: An Alternative View." *Brewery History* 169 (2017): 73–76.

———. "Gruit: Nothing Mysterious About It." *Lost Beers* (blog), July 13, 2017. http://lostbeers.com/gruit-nothing-mysterious-about-it/.

NatureGate. Accessed April 2018. www.luontoportti.com/suomi/en/kasvit/. This website is devoted to wild plants, birds, butterflies, and fishes.

Nelson, Max. *The Barbarian's Beverage: A History of Beer in Ancient Europe*. Abingdon, England: Routledge, 2005.

———. "The Geography of Beer in Europe from 1000 BC to AD 1000." In *The Geography of Beer: Regions, Environment, and Society*, edited by Mark Patterson and Nancy Hoalst-Pullen, 9–21. Dordrecht, Netherlands: Springer, 2014.

Nordland, Odd. *Brewing and Beer Traditions in Norway: The Social Anthropological Background of the Brewing Industry*. Oslo: Norwegian Research Council for Science and the Humanities, 1969.

Palmer, John. *How to Brew: Everything You Need to Know to Brew Great Beer Every Time*. Boulder, CO: Brewers Publications, 2017.

Pálsson, Hermann, and Paul Edwards, trans. *Orkneyinga Saga: The History of the Earls of Orkney*. London: Penguin Classics, 1981.

Papazian, Charlie. *Microbrewed Adventures: A Lupulin-Filled Journey to the Heart and Flavor of the World's Great Craft Beers*. New York: HarperCollins Publishers, 2005.

Preiss, Richard, Caroline Tyrawa, Kristoffer Krogerus, Lars Marius Garshol, and George van der Merwe. "Traditional Norwegian Kveik Are a Genetically Distinct Group of Domesticated *Saccharomyces cerevisiae* Brewing Yeasts." *Frontiers in Microbiology* 9 (2018). https://doi.org/10.3389/fmicb.2018.02137.

Price, T. Douglas. *Ancient Scandinavia: An Archaeological History from the First Humans to the Vikings*. New York: Oxford University Press, 2015.

Ränk, Gustav. *Vanha Viro: Kansa ja kulttuuri*. Helsinki: Finnish Literature Society, 1955.

Räsänen, Matti. *Ohrasta olutta, rukiista ryypättävää: Mietojen kansanomaisten viljajuomien valmistus Suomessa*. Jyväskylä, Finland: University of Jyväskylä, 1977.

———. *Savokarjalainen ateria*. Helsinki: Otava, 1980.

———. "Vom Halm zum Fass: Die Volkstümlichen alkoholarmen Getreide-getränke in Finnland." PhD diss., Suomen Muinaismuistoyhdistys, 1975.

Rasmussen, Truls C. "Characterization of Genotype and Beer Fermentation Properties of Norwegian Farmhouse Ale Yeasts." Master's thesis, Norwegian University of Science and Technology, 2016.

Räty, Antti. BeerFinland.com. Accessed April 2018. www.beerfinland.com. This website is devoted to Finnish brewery history.

Roesdahl, Else. *The Vikings*. New York: Penguin Random House, 2018.

Sallinen-Gimpi, Pirkko. *Karjalainen keittokirja*. Helsinki: Tammi, 2000.

Salomonsson, Anders. *Gotlandsdricka: Traditionell kultur som regional identitetssymbol*. Karlstad, Sweden: Press' Förlag AB, 1979.

Seppänen-Pora, Irja. *Apposkaalista mantsikkamöllöön: Karjalan kannaksen kansanruoka*. Helsinki: Otava, 1979.

Serra, Daniel, and Hanna Tunberg. *An Early Meal: A Viking Age Cookbook & Culinary Odyssey*. Furulund, Sweden: ChronoCopia Publishing, 2013.

Sirelius, Uuno. *Suomen kansanomaista kulttuuria: Esineellisen kansatieteen tuloksia 1*. Helsinki: Otava, 1919.

Sloth, Pernille R., Ulla Lund Hansen, and Sabine Karg. "Viking Age Garden Plants from Southern Scandinavia—Diversity, Taphonomy and Cultural Aspects." *Danish Journal of Archaeology* 1, no. 1 (2012): 27–38.

Sysilä, Ilkka. *Small-Scale Brewing*. Self-published, 1997.

Talve, Ilmar. *Finnish Folk Culture*. Helsinki: Finnish Literature Society, 2012.

Thibault, Martin. "Breaking Bread with Seto Õlu: Uncovering a Forgotten Kingdom's Brewing Tradition." *BeerAdvocate Magazine* 121, February 2017.

Tikkanen, Unto. *Viinin ja oluen lähteillä*. Helsinki: Tammi, 2004.

Unger, Richard W. *Beer in the Middle Ages and the Renaissance*. Philadelphia: University of Pennsylvania Press, 2007.

Vanhanen, Santeri, and Satu Koivisto. "Pre-Roman Iron Age Settlement Continuity and Cereal Cultivation in Coastal Finland as Shown by Multiproxy Evidence at Bäljars 2 Site in SW Finland." *Journal of Archaeological Science: Reports* 1 (March 2015): 38–52.

Vehviläinen, Olli. *Hiivan tarina: Suomen leivinhiivateollisuuden vaiheet 1885–1970*. Pori, Finland: Suomen hiivatehtaitten myyntiyhdistys, 1970.

Verberg, Susan. "The Rise and Fall of Gruit." Self-published e-book, 2018. Via www.academia.edu.

Vilkuna, Kustaa H. J. *Juomareiden valtakunta: Suomalaisten känni ja kulttuuri 1500–1850*. Helsinki: Teos, 2015.

Vuorela, Toivo. *Suomalainen kansankulttuuri*. Helsinki: WSOY, 1975.

White, Chris, and Jamil Zainasheff. *Yeast: The Practical Guide to Beer Fermentation*. Boulder, CO: Brewers Publications, 2010.

Winroth, Anders. *The Age of the Vikings*. Princeton, NJ: Princeton University Press, 2014.

Zimmerman, Jereme. *Brew Beer Like a Yeti: Traditional Techniques and Recipes for Unconventional Ales, Gruits, and Other Ferments Using Minimal Hops*. White River Junction, VT: Chelsea Green Publishing, 2018.

INDEX

Page numbers in *italics* indicate photos

acetic acid bacteria, 122
Achillea millefolium. See yarrow
Adam of Bremen, 48
aeration, 178
agriculture, 37–38
alcohol by volume (ABV), 13
alcohol content
    of feast ales, 5, 95
    of kaimiškas, 31
    low-alcohol ales, 5–6, 95–105
    measurement of, 13
    of medieval ales, 190
    of sahti, 5–6, 22, 62–63, 68, 119
    social status and, 53, 209
alderwood, 117
ale, etymology of, 56–57
Ale Apothecary, 92
Ale, Beer, and Brewsters in England
        (Bennett), 50–51
ankur casks, *161*
Arney, Paul, 92

bacteria
    acetic acid bacteria, 122
    lactic bacteria, 33, 71, 103, 122,
        171, 179
    and souring of beer, 45–46,
        127–128, 158
baker's yeast, *126*
    commercial production of, 9,
        126–127
    origins of, 121
    for sahti, 9, 23, 64, 123, 127–128
    souring bacteria in, 71, 103,
        127–128, 179
Baltic regions, 6–8, *7*

Barbarian's Beverage, The (Nelson), 48
barley and barley malt, *108, 111*
    in boza, 104
    characteristics of, 110
    cultivation of, 37
    heirloom varieties, 41
    importance of, 109
    in sahti, 84, 90, 194
barrels, wooden, 43
beer
    earliest fermented drinks, 38–39,
        95–96
    use of term, 56–57, 96
Beer (Cornell), 45, 46
*Beer in the Middle Ages and the Re-
        naissance* (Unger), 45
beer porridge, *94*, 95
Belgian lambics, 46, 122
Belgian saison, 32–33
Bennett, Judith, 50–51
bere malt, 41
beta glucans, 110
bière de garde, 32–33
birch-bark buckets, *39*
birch smoke, 117
BJ's Restaurant & Brewhouse, 93
boar's saliva, 122
bog myrtle (*Myrica gale*), *139, 185*
    in Iron Age ales, 49
    in medieval ales, 184–186, 189
    recommended amounts of, 189
    safety concerns about, 184–185
    in sahti, 138–139
    in Viking ales, 190
boiling process, 10, 43–44, 142,
        149–152, 177–178